AMERICAN POPULAR HISTORY AND CULTURE

edited by
JEROME NADELHAFT
UNIVERSITY OF MAINE

A ROUTLEDGE SERIES

Race-ing Masculinity
Identity in Contemporary U.S. Men's Writing

John Christopher Cunningham

ROUTLEDGE
NEW YORK & LONDON

Published in 2002 by
Routledge
29 West 35th Street
New York, NY 10001
www.routledge-ny.com

Published in Great Britain by
Routledge
11 New Fetter Lane
London EC4P 4EE

Routledge is an imprint of the Taylor & Francis Group.

Copyright © 2002 by Routledge.

All rights reserved. No part of this book may be reprinted or reproduced or utilized in any form or by any electronic, mechanical, or other means, now known or hereafter invented, including photocopying and recording, or in any information storage or retrieval system, without written permission from the publishers.

10 9 8 7 6 5 4 3

Library of Congress Cataloging-in-Publication Data

Cunningham, John Christopher, 1964–
    Race-ing masculinity : identity in contemporary U. S. men's writing / by John Christopher Cunningham
    p. cm. — (American popular history and culture)
    Includes bibliographical references and index.
    ISBN 0-415-93476-1
    1. American literature—Male authors-History and criticism. 2. American literature—20th century—History and criticism. 3. Identity (Psychology) in literature. 4. Masculinity in literature. 5. Race in literature. 6. Men in literature. I. Title: Identity in contemporary U.S. men's writing. II. Title: identity in contemporary United States men's writing. III. Title. IV. garland studies in American popular history and culture.

PS153.M3 C86 2002
810.9'353—dc21
                                                                                                                                2002017784

Printed on acid-free, 250 year-life paper
Manufactured in the United States of America

To Mom and Dad

CONTENTS

Acknowledgments   ix

Chapter One   1
Introduction: Literature as a Site for the
Constitution and Reconfiguration of Identity

Chapter Two   15
"This Thing Going With My Bride
to Straighten Out in America"

Chapter Three   41
Hegemony and the Broad Celebration
of Charles Johnson

Chapter Four   69
"Hey, Mr. Liberace Will You Vote for Zeta?":
Looking for the *Joto* in Chicano Men's
Autobiographical Writing

Chapter Five   95
"His Complexion was of a Tone
I Want to Call Flesh-Colored"

Bibliography   113

Index   117

ACKNOWLEDGMENTS

David, I can't thank you enough; the best thing I can tell you is, "It's done!" Shelley Streeby, you make me do right, think right, feel safe. Dwight, you've got to live with the man you've helped me become; I love you. Alycee, you are the closest thing to a role model in my life—smart, fine and true. Rachel, Mary Pat, Mike: you're the best minds a dissertation writer could bump up against. Katherine King and Kim Crenshaw, you signal a good new day in this profession. Val Smith, I thank you for your crucial help in my project. King-Kok Cheung, this whole thing began with a class on Asian American literature. I will never be able to thank you enough for the direction you've given me. Vince Pecora, your "tough love" has been my biggest support throughout my graduate career, just as your criticism has been the strongest inspiration in my writing process. Thank you. Finally, to the New Jersey crew that helped me get through the revisions, I love you all: Gerry Smith-Wright, Theresa Green, Jennifer Schmidt, Jennifer Holly, Diya Abdo, and my sweet Tim.

Race-ing Masculinity

CHAPTER ONE

Introduction:
Literature as a Site for the Constitution and Reconfiguration of Identity

The following book consists of a set of essays on contemporary U.S. male writers. My focus on male writers grew out of the concern, expressed by a number of male writers of color, that their voices were being systematically silenced. Ishmael Reed and Frank Chin, for example, have argued that support for the writing of women of color by academia and the publishing industry constitutes a White supremacist attempt to silence men of color. While I do believe that, in a college literature course, one is more likely to read something by Toni Morrison, Maxine Hong Kingston, Leslie Marmon Silko, or Sandra Cisneros than anything by a contemporary male African American, Asian American, American Indian or Chicano/Latino writer, I don't believe Reed's and Chin's diagnosis is correct. What seems more likely is that the presence in most English Departments of a strong feminist sensibility has raised interest in women-authored texts and has created reservations about arguably sexist texts by writers like Reed and Chin. If, however, it is true that the voices of contemporary men of color are less frequently taught in literature courses, for whatever reason, I believe it is necessary to explore why, committed as I am to a pluralist pedagogy.

I examine work by male writers not to find out what "real" men think and feel, but to see how literature by men represents them. Literature is one mode of writing among many putting forward ideas about what men have been and what they can be. In its highly crafted form, it offers an ideal site for the generation and dissemination of ideas about gender and race. It also offers a particularly clear arena for the kinds of articulations and rearticulations through which identity is produced and changed.

I draw my position on the constitution of identity from the work of self-defined "post-Marxist" cultural critics, Chantal Mouffe and Ernesto Laclau. In their writings, together and separately, Laclau and Mouffe lay out a theory of "radical democracy" based on the notion that the political world functions through the constant rearticulation of blocs of identity: a process they call "hegemony." One can trace the genealogical line of their concept of identity to French Marxist Louis Althusser's work on subjectivity. In his early book, *Politics and Ideology in Marxist Theory*, Laclau writes that "Althusser's most important and specific contribution to the study of ideology" is "the conception that the basic function of all ideology is to interpellate/constitute individuals as subjects."[1] It is the process of "interpellation" or "hailing" that will take a central place in all of Laclau's later work.

Althusser's well-known early piece, "Ideology and Ideological State Apparatuses," begins a search for the "ideological" by first distinguishing "between concrete individuals on the one hand and concrete subjects on the other."[2] He explains:

> ideology "acts" or "functions" in such a way that it "recruits" subjects among the individuals (it recruits them all), or "transforms" the individuals into subjects (it transforms them all) by that very precise operation which I have called *interpellation* or hailing. ("I,"174)

It is in this sense that Althusser claims that the "existence of ideology and the hailing or interpellation of individuals as subjects are one and the same thing" ("I,"175).

The term "individual" here refers not to a position of total undifferentiation, but to that of a person existing within structures of differentiation, but who is, in a sense, unconscious of them, or, unselfconscious. A state of actual undifferentiation is only an abstract, theoretical position, since distinguishing categories pre-exist all persons. What is important and new in Althusser's argument is his claim that the second position—that of subjectivity—is similarly abstract. Althusser writes:

> ideology has always-already interpellated individuals as subjects, which amounts to making it clear that individuals are always—already interpellated by ideology as subjects, which necessarily leads us to one last proposition: individuals are always-already subjects. Hence individuals are "abstract" with respect to the subjects which they always-already are. ("I,"175-6)

Althusser demonstrates by example how this proposition functions:

> an individual is always-already a subject, even before he is born...it is certain in advance that it will bear its Father's Name, and will therefore have an identity and be irreplaceable. Before its birth, the child is therefore always-already a subject, appointed as a subject in and by the specific familial ideological configuration in which it is "expected" once it has been conceived. ("I,"176)

In the end, Althusser offers the binary, individual/subject, only to deconstruct it as a starting point for conceptualizing subjectivity in a way which asserts the ultimate social constructedness of identity: there is no individual or subject "before" socialization.

The strength of Althusser's formulation does not lie, however, in his "social conditioning" argument (similar arguments are age-old); rather, his innovation rests in the observation that socialization is carried out through a process of interpellation or "hailing" as he calls it, which, even as it creates subjectivity, also creates in the subject a sense that her/his subjectivity preexists this subjectivizing moment. The error comes when one believes that the interpellating or identity-forming call acknowledges an already existing essential identity; that is, when the "recognition" of the hailing acts to validate the feeling that one's identity is fully-formed and "already there." The recognition, however, is really a *mis*recognition of identity as stable and preexistent, since it is exactly such moments, enacted even before one's birth, that create a differentiated sense of identity. This misrecognition becomes "ideological" when it acts to "naturalize" one's identity, and thus one's beliefs and desires (i.e. one's ideological orientation). Althusser writes:

> those who are in ideology believe themselves by definition outside ideology: one of the effects of ideology is the practical denegation of the ideological character of ideology by ideology. ("I," 175)

To illustrate crudely, in the moment that someone says, "Hey, little girl," the person so hailed recognizes herself in the call, recognizes that she is a "little girl," with all that this term entails. This moment is ideological in nature because it feels to her like proof or confirmation that she is, and already was, a "little girl," whereas, in truth, it is only the infinite similar moments of hailing which make this person imagine herself to really be a "little girl," with all that this term entails.

Laclau, emphasizing, for his part, the psychological character of interpellation, embraces it as the starting point for his work:

> the concept of "interpellation" is the phenomenon of "identification" which Freud described at various points of his work, especially in *Group Psychology*. In its Lacanian reformulation, it presupposes the centrality of the category of "lack." In my own analyses, the important issue is also the reconstitution of shattered political identities through new forms of identification.[3]

Following Althusser, Laclau recognizes the central functioning of misrecognition in subject formation, writing, "through interpellation individuals live their conditions of existence as if they were the autonomous principle of the latter—as if they, the determinate, constituted the determinant" (*PI*, 101). In other words:

> *Individuals*, who are simple bearers of structures, are transformed by ideology into *subjects*, that is to say, that they live the relation with their real conditions of existence as if they themselves were the

autonomous principle of determination of that relation. The mechanism of this characteristic inversion is interpellation. (*PI*,100)

Once the ontological status of subjectivity has been problematized by the phenomenon of misrecognition, Laclau insists that the task of analyzing "the ideological level of a determinate social formation" must turn from individuals within a formation to "the interpellative structures which constitute it" (*PI*,102). This is the point at which Laclau breaks with Althusser.

Because, in "Ideology and Ideological State Apparatuses," Althusser works from the position that the economic relations of production determine ideology in the last instance, he supports the absolute agency of institutions and the corresponding passivity of individuals interpellated by those institutions. For Laclau, on the other hand, moving away from stable notions of subjective agency does not mean moving toward a stable notion of institutional agency. Laclau refuses to accept the complete determinacy of the economy and its superstructural institutions in subject formation, arguing that while it is true that subjects arise only under conditions of interpellation, interpellative structures likewise can only be said to exist when individual subjects collectively constitute them. He writes:

> interpellation is the terrain for the production of discourse...in order to "produce" subjects successfully, the latter must identify with it. The Althusserian emphasis on interpellation as a functional mechanism in social reproduction does not leave enough space to study the construction of subjects from the point of view of the individuals receiving those interpellations. (NR,210)

Laclau supplements Althusser's notion of institutions with an assertion of activity on the part of subjects, again by invoking the psychological character of interpellation. He writes:

> the incorporation of the individual into the symbolic order occurs through *identifications*. The individual is not simply an identity within the structure but is transformed by it into a subject, and this requires acts of identification. (NR,211)

The relation Laclau attempts to establish between subjects and institutions does not, it must be stressed, deny the active role of institutions. Laclau writes:

> institutions are fully present in our approach...we have asserted that social agents are *partially* internal to the institutions, thus forcing both the notion of "agency" and "institution" to be deconstructed...the agents are not just blind instruments or bearers of structures for the simple reason that the latter do not constitute a closed system, but are riven with antagonisms, threatened by a constitutive outside and merely have a weak or relative form of integration....In opposition to

the postulation of two *separate* metaphysical entities—agents and structures—we suggest the following: (a) that there are merely relative *degrees* of institutionalization of the social, which penetrate and define the subjectivity of the agents themselves; and (b) that the institutions do not constitute closed structural frameworks, but loosely integrated complexes requiring the constant intervention of articulatory practices. (NR,223-4)

For Laclau, the reconstruction of interpellative structures involves confronting the mutual constitutivity of subjects and interpellators: it involves conceptualizing interpellation as an interchange between subjects and institutions, rather than as a function of either by itself, of the economy, or of other "grounded" forces. Laclau writes:

It's not a question of "someone" or "something" producing an effect of transformation or articulation, as if its identity was somehow previous to this effect. Rather, the production of the effect is part of the construction of the identity of the agent producing it…one cannot ask *who* the agent of hegemony is, but *how* someone becomes the subject through hegemonic articulation instead. (NR,210-1)

Laclau's work is thus "poststructuralist" in the sense that he accepts that some structuration of social relations is necessary to render them intelligible, but denies any permanence or ultimate "reliability" to any structuration. He writes:

The social is not only the infinite play of differences. It is also the attempt to limit that play, to domesticate infinitude, to embrace it within the finitude of an order. But this order—or structure—no longer takes the form of an underlying essence of the social; rather, it is an attempt—by definition unstable and precarious—to act over that "social," to *hegemonize* it. (NR,91)

In another formulation:

the systematic element, its cohesiveness, does not have the status of a ground…insofar as the social "order" does exist, there is a constitutive outside which deforms and threatens the "system" and this very fact means that the latter can only have the status of a *hegemonic* attempt at articulation, not a ground…while this doesn't mean depriving social practices of *all* their coherence, it nevertheless does mean denying that this coherence can have the rationalistic status of a superhard "transcendentality." (NR,214)

Once society is understood to function, like all systems, through partial or "contingent" structurations, the political task thus becomes the formulation of strategies appropriate for decentered subjects and ungrounded interpellative (i.e. social) forces. This task is the goal of Laclau's collaborative work with Chantal Mouffe.

Acknowledging the ambiguity constitutive of the process of subjectification, Mouffe and Laclau write in *Hegemony and Marxist Strategy* that subjects cannot "be the origin of social relations...as all 'experience' depends on precise discursive conditions of possibility."[4] On the other hand, they recognize that any "precise discursive conditions" cannot be described without reference to the subjects which identify with and give voice to a given discourse. Their work thus seeks to define the conditions under which subjects are created by and reciprocally create interpellative structures. Laclau and Mouffe name the mutual constitution of subjects and interpellating discourses as "articulation." In their schema, Althusser's "institutions" are recast as "discursive formations," a term derived from Michel Foucault. In his study, *The Archaeology of Knowledge*, Foucault conceptualizes socializing forces or institutions as "discourses" in order to demonstrate their ideological character without grounding them in any transcendental force such the economy, Nature or God. Foucault locates these discourses in historical documents—not as discreetly articulated wholes, however, but as signifiers dispersed across a variety of statements. These signifiers may be said to constitute a "discourse" once they have been abstractly reconstructed in a totality defined not by their *a priori* stylistic or thematic connection, but by their recurrence alone.

Mouffe and Laclau adopt Foucault's theory of discursive formations, modifying it chiefly by stressing the *regularity* of the dispersion of signifiers in a discourse and by challenging Foucault's distinction between discursive and non-discursive objects. They write:

> The type of coherence we attribute to a discursive formation is...close to that which characterizes the concept of "discursive formation" formulated by Foucault: regularity in dispersion...Foucault makes dispersion itself the principle of unity...the discursive formation can also be seen from the perspective of the *regularity* in dispersion, and be thought, in that sense, as an ensemble of differential positions. This ensemble...constitutes a configuration, which in certain contexts of exteriority can be *signified* as a totality. (H,105-6)

The regularity of the formation lends it, and the "reality" it signifies, a relative stability. They write:

> there have to be partial fixations—otherwise, the very flow of differences would be impossible...the social does not manage to fix itself in the intelligible and instituted forms of a *society*, the social only exists...as an effort to construct that impossible object. Any discourse is constituted as an attempt to dominate the field of discursivity, to arrest the flow of differences, to construct a centre. We will call the privileged discursive points of this partial fixation, *nodal points* [following Lacan] *points de capiton*...privileged signifiers that fix the meaning of a signifying chain. This limitation of the productivity of the

Introduction

> signifying chain establishes the positions that make predication possible. (H,112)

Laclau and Mouffe's work is only comprehensible through a poststructuralist orientation in which "all discourse of fixation becomes metaphorical" (*H*,111).

In a move which has the effect of naming as an ideological effect Althusser's elimination of individual agency by the economy, Laclau extends the definition of ideology from the *self*-misrecognition of subjects to the misrecognition of any identity or state of being as permanent and immutable. From the standpoint of a politics of hegemony, he writes:

> The ideological would not consist of the misrecognition of a positive essence, but exactly the opposite: it would consist of the non-recognition of the precarious character of any positivity, of the impossibility of any ultimate suture. The ideological would consist of those discursive forms through which a society tries to institute itself as such on the basis of closure, of the fixation of meaning, of the non-recognition of the infinite play of differences. The ideological would be the will to "totality" of any totalizing discourse. And insofar as the social is impossible without some fixation of meaning, without the discourse of closure, the ideological must be seen as constitutive of the social. The social only exists as the vain attempt to institute that impossible object: society. Utopia is the essence of any communication and social practice. (NR,92)

The assertion of the ontological ambiguity of any social reality is Mouffe and Laclau's second modification of Foucault. They write:

> Our analysis rejects the distinction between discursive and non-discursive practices...every object is constituted as an object of discourse, insofar as no object is given outside every discursive condition of emergence. (H,107)

Statements like this have generated much criticism of Mouffe and Laclau's project. Numerous traditional critics, especially traditional Marxists, have accused them of denying the existence of any reality outside human mediation. Such accusations, however, arise from a misunderstanding of a premise in their work which is not as radical as it may at first seem. For Laclau and Mouffe, denying the existence of objects outside discourse is a matter of definition, since by the term "object," they designate a material or abstract "thing" which has been marked out by some sort of signification. They write:

> The fact that every object is constituted as an object of discourse has *nothing to do* with whether there is a world external to thought, or with the realism/idealism opposition. An earthquake or the falling of a brick is an event that certainly exists, in the sense that it occurs here and now, independently of my will. But whether their specificity as

> objects is constructed in terms of "natural phenomena" or "expressions of the wrath of God," depends upon the structuring of a discursive field. What is denied is not that such objects exist externally to thought, but the rather different assertion that they could constitute themselves as objects outside any discursive condition of emergence. (H,108)

Laclau reemphasizes this point in a later interview:

> At no time have we asserted that "material objects do not possess an identity outside of any differential context"...material objects have an existence independent of any differential context. That's why we have insisted on the historicity of the being of objects, and have deliberately distinguished that being from their mere existence. (NR,217-8)

The rejection of non-discursive objectivity is an important move, for, in the absence of any underlying "truth," ideas of "being" and "identity" can be apprehended as free of final determination, a reorientation which opens up both a new position from which to analyze ideology and the possibility of political change through active rearticulation of identities.

Because identities are not finally determined by any transcendental force, they are subject to reconstitution through new discursive forms. Mouffe and Laclau write:

> the open and incomplete character of every social identity permits its articulation to different historico-discursive formulations—that is to "blocs" in the sense of Sorel and Gramsci. (H,114)

In order to use this insight to the advantage of radical democratic objectives, Laclau and Mouffe explore the way discourses recruit subjects, or (which is the same thing) the way subjects identify with discourses. They argue that in order for a discursive formation to come into existence as an interpellating force, it must not only assemble a set of regularly dispersed signifiers, but must also collect enough subjects, (mis)recognizing in themselves, or identifying with, its signifying "nodal points," to cohere and disseminate itself. In other words, a hegemonic discourse must provide a set of signifiers compatible with or more powerful than other, already existing identities of a great and dispersed enough number of subjects in order to survive. Laclau writes:

> The centrality and credibility gained by a discourse in a particular society depends on its ability to extend its argumentative fabric in a number of directions, all of which converge in a hegemonic configuration. (NR,244)

The shared identity which results from this mass identification creates a sense of equivalence, or "hegemony," between otherwise heterogeneous subjects.

Equivalential discourses do not, however, simply emphasize similarities; they also suppress their subjects' differences. "Hence," Laclau and Mouffe write:

> the ambiguity penetrating every relation of equivalence: two terms, to be equivalent, must be different—otherwise, there would be a simple identity. On the other hand, the equivalence exists only through the act of subverting the differential character of those terms. (*H*,128)

Discursive formations create mythic group identities in radically different individuals insofar as they are able to highlight similarities between those individuals, while simultaneously masking their differences. A successful hegemonic discourse must therefore find ways to bracket all signifiers which would engender doubt in the minds of its members as to the accuracy or fullness of their identifications with others in the group.

Locating the exclusionary principle of a discourse is not a simple task, however. Logical consistency, for example, provides no clue as to what is excluded, since discourses are not constructed "logically," in a strict sense. Laclau writes:

> There are different types of interpellations (political, religious, familial, etc.) which coexist whilst being articulated within an ideological discourse in a relative unity...By unity we must not necessarily understand logical consistency—on the contrary, the ideological unity of a discourse is perfectly compatible with a wide margin of logical inconsistency. (*PI*,102)

Foucault demonstrates how regularity of dispersion provides limits to a discourse. What marks off the boundary of the dispersion, however, remains unexplained in Foucault's work. Laclau and Mouffe's answer to the question of delimitation lies in the assertion that a discursive formation "will assume coherence through its opposition to that which denies it" (*NR*,219).

They put forward the notion of "constitutive exteriority" to explain how discursive formations can partially fix identity. Mouffe and Laclau write, "Every 'society' constitutes its own forms of rationality and intelligibility by dividing itself; that is by expelling outside itself any surplus of meaning subverting it" (*H*,136-7). In the "ungrounded" or "decentered" terrain on which hegemony functions, all identity is relational. Any partial fixation of identity must therefore be articulated against a contrarily defined exteriority. Only the articulation of what an identity is not allows its "positive" emergence. In hegemony, however, the process is complicated by the fact that the bloc is composed of various and contradictory individuals. Their heterogeneity prevents the emergence of a "natural" common antagonist. It is only the effacement of difference through the process of condensation that allows for the articulation of a collective exteriority.

Laclau explains that the cohesion of a hegemonic bloc occurs according to "the ability of each interpellative element to fulfill a role of condensation with respect to the others":

> when each of these isolated interpellations operates as a *symbol* of the others, we have a relatively unified ideological discourse. (*PI*,102)

Laclau borrows the concept of condensation from psychoanalysis, defined by Jean Laplanche and J. B. Pontalis as the process in which "a single representation represents in itself many associative chains at the intersection of which it is situated" (quoted in *PI*,93). In a hegemonic discourse, a single term, for example, becomes the site of a condensation in which the specificity of the individual nodal points is effaced. The central term holds the entire discourse together by subsuming the other nodal terms through a process of metaphorization. They partially lose their differentiated meaning as they come to stand as symbols of the central nodal term. That term, in its condensed form, affirms the positivity of the entire formation in contradiction to, or better, by negating, the "outside," which, in its turn, reciprocally negates the former's identity. Through this double act of negation, the antagonistic nodal point provides coherence to both its own discourse and its constitutive outside by defining them as polarities. A perhaps overdue example would undoubtedly help at this point.

As a rather crude illustration, I will consider the constitution of the discourse of contemporary Latino identity. The nodal points of this discourse might include "brown skin," Spanish-speaking ability, residence in the United States, Latin American ancestry, etc. The discourse interpellates individuals who identify with these signifiers as Latino subjects. The term "Latino" may be said to operate as the antagonistic nodal point, for it overdetermines all the other nodal points through its negation of the exteriority of "Whiteness" or "Angloness," which, through racist articulatory practices, reciprocally negates it. The adjectives "Latino" and "White"/"Anglo" gain their meaning through their negative relationship to each other. The strength of the condensation around the term "Latino" is proportional to the degree of negativity, exercised by both verbal and material practices, directed at those defined as Latinos. As the antagonistic pressure of White domination increases, signifiers of non-racial differences lose their "literal" meaning and are aligned through their ability to stand in as substitutions for the term "Latino"—that is, as symbols of resistance to White supremacy ("brown skin" thus becomes not a simple marker of color, but metaphorizes "Latinoness" in its opposition to white skin, Spanish language symbolizes antagonism to White hegemony, etc.).

The anti-racist condensation around the term "Latino" is the precondition for the emergence of Latino identity. White domination as such can only be resisted if the discourse antagonistic to it not only coalesces around nodal points compatible with a large and dispersed subject group, but also if the heterogeneity of that group and the nodal points themselves are simultaneously disguised. Any discourse is threatened by the surplus of meanings embodied by its subjects. The discourse of Latinoness omits any number of signifiers (dealing with, for example, gender, class, sexuality, etc.) which are equally pertinent markers of its subjects' identities but might make them understand themselves in distinction to other Latinos. Only the condensation prevents this heterogeneity from disarticulating the discourse. The recent and growing successes of Latinos in Los Angeles politics, for one example, attest to the success of the condensation around the term "Latino."

While Laclau and Mouffe acknowledge this "politics of difference" as constitutive of all hegemony, their radical democratic objectives emphasize another aspect of hegemonization. Rather than simply supporting the domination of the hegemonic field by stagnant antagonistic nodal points, Laclau and Mouffe support the incorporation of new nodal terms in order to expand the hegemonizing capacity of egalitarian discourses. In some cases, this may entail rearticulating the central antagonistic term itself. Their objective is to expand the horizon of hegemonization rather than simply controlling an already interpellated group.

To return to the case of Latino identity, the rearticulation of the term "Latino" as the more gender inclusive term "Latino/a," or more radically, "Latina/o," extends the number of identities subject to hegemonization, because its defining point of antagonism asserts the positivity of individuals negated by the practices of a White supremacist and patriarchal exteriority. While a linguistic gesture will not alone eradicate concrete gender inequalities exerted on or from within the Latino community, it will nevertheless hegemonize more effectively Latinas whose interpellation by the discourse of Latino identity has been partially disarticulated by discourses opposing sexism in their communities, and will reorganize the meaning of (male) Latino gender identity in less dominating ways. One could even argue that by creating an antagonism to several different forms of subordination, the discursive expansion carried out by the rearticulation of the term "Latina/o" moves in the even broader direction of radical democracy, which is antagonistic to all forms of subordination. Discursive rearticulations such as this are the practical side of Mouffe and Laclau's politics, and, I would argue, the precondition of all political change.

I should reiterate that the discursive recasting of practical political struggles does not render them any less "real" or important. Laclau and Mouffe simply claim that political struggle only emerges between contrarily articulated hegemonic blocs. Laclau characterizes social struggles as "'wars of interpretations' in which the very meaning of demands is discursively constructed through struggle" (*NR*,216). The hegemonic construction of group identity is for Laclau and Mouffe the simultaneous construction of that group's "interests." They claim that "political practice constructs the interests it represents" (*H*,120). But none of this to say that there are not "real" conflicts outside of language between different people. Mouffe and Laclau's claim is, rather, that outside of discourse, collective struggle cannot emerge. Resistance to domination cannot be organized on the level of groups, or even be imagined as group struggle, without a hegemonic discourse. Laclau writes, "However abstract and general 'needs' may be, their articulation will always occur within specific discursive practices" (NR,218). Inequalities and subordination may abstractly be said to preexist discursive representations of them, but the interest in changing them and the means to carry out these changes must be articulated, and be articulated effectively if they are to proceed.

Literature by men is a location where needs, inequalities, and arguments for change find articulation. The framework Mouffe and Laclau lay out thus offers multiple uses for my project. Their theorization first of all places articulation at the center of the politics of identity. Secondly, because they are contingent, all articulations are subject to critique, challenge, revision, and supplementation. Literary criticism thus becomes, among other things, a possible site for engaging in a radical democratic rearticulation of the various discourses functioning in texts.

In my second chapter, I look at the how the articulation of Asian American identity in the works of several Asian American male writers, while presenting itself as genderless, has a strong masculinist, if not sexist, bias which limits its value for Asian American women and queer people and, consequently, for the community as a whole. Starting with Frank Chin, whose gender politics have been rather widely discussed, I look back at a classic work of Asian American literature, John Okada's *No-No Boy*, to suggest a genealogy of masculinist conceptions of Asian American identity. Finally, I move to Shawn Hsu Wong's *Homebase* to demonstrate how the articulation of the history of male Asian immigration can orient the articulation of Asian American identity within a masculinist framework.

My third chapter looks at the work of the African American writer Charles Johnson. I consider the growing critical interest in Johnson's work in the context of the conflicting interplay of discourses of feminism and male supremacy in his novels, and examine the relationship between this vision of gender and the conservatism of Johnson's articulation of race issues.

My fourth chapter adds the discourse of "perverse" sexuality more directly to the dissertation. I examine a possible countertradition of the "joto," or queer, in "canonized" Chicano novels from Jose Antonio Villareal to Arturo Islas. More specifically, I note, through readings of Richard Rodriguez's and Oscar Zeta Acosta's autobiographical work, the interplay of homosocial sexual politics with their respective conservative and revolutionary takes on race issues.

In preparing my dissertation for publication as a book, I have added a final planned chapter on Don DeLillo's *White Noise*. I consider it vital, in a schematically multiethnic project such as my own, to include White cultural productions. As I argue in this chapter, omitting mention of Whiteness and its cultural effects only strengthens the enormous political power it exerts over all our lives. Specifically, I look at the way the reception and dissemination of this novel as a hallmark of "the postmodern condition" has the perhaps unintended effect of rendering non-White representations of contemporary life more marginal, less important.

I end my introduction with a final note about my focus on male writers. Given the priority historically granted to the cultural products of men, one can understand the increased study of women as the long overdue cultural "equal treatment" of women. On the other hand, men of color cannot stand in for the block of male writers who have historically displaced women's texts from full consideration. Indeed, male writers of color have been subject to their own history of marginalization and silencing.

Feminism, moreover, has always argued that its objectives for liberation require not only the rediscovery and revaluation of women's culture, but also the critique of men's culture. Black feminist literary critic bell hooks, for example, calls for ongoing reading and response to men's writing:

> If we are ever to construct a feminist movement that is not based on the premise that men and women are always at war with one another, then we must be willing to acknowledge the appropriateness of complex critical responses to writing by men even if it is sexist. Clearly women can learn from writers whose work is sexist, even be inspired by it, because sexism may be simply one dimension of that work. Concurrently, fiercely critiquing the sexism does not mean that one does not value the work.[5]

Indeed, it does no disservice to male writers to critique their writing; the effort of critique testifies to the relevance of their thought. Besides, as hooks suggests in her brief article, "Feminist Focus on Men: a Comment," to avoid addressing the work of men means to rob feminist work of much of its power:

> it is essential for the transformation of gender roles, of society that the exploited and oppressed speak to and among ourselves, but it is equally essential that we address without fear those who exploit, oppress, and dominate us. If women remain unable to speak to and about men in a feminist voice then our challenge to male domination on other fronts is seriously undermined.[6]

It is in this spirit that I proceed.

Notes

1. Ernesto Laclau, *Politics and Ideology in Marxist Theory* (London: Verso, 1977), 100. Further references are cited in the text with the abbreviation *PI*.
2. Louis Althusser, "Ideology and Ideological State Apparatuses (Notes Toward an Investigation)" in *Lenin and Philosophy and Other Essays* (New York: Monthly Review Press, 1971), 174. Further references are cited in the text with the abbreviation "I."
3. Ernesto Laclau, *New Reflections of the Revolution of Our Time* (London: Verso, 1990), 186. Further references are cited in the text with the abbreviation *NR*.
4. Ernesto Laclau and Chantal Mouffe, *Hegemony and Socialist Strategy* (Verso: London, 1985), 115. Further references are cited in text with the abbreviation *H*.
5. bell hooks, "Representations: Feminism and Black Masculinity," in *Yearning: Race, Gender, and Cultural Politics* (Boston: South End Press, 1991), 66.
6. bell hooks, "Feminist Focus on Men: A Comment," in *Talking Back* (South End Press, Boston: 1989), 129-30.

CHAPTER TWO

"This Thing Going With My Bride to Straighten Out in America"

The work of Chinese American writer Frank Chin has been especially hard for me to come to terms with; even as it is the most forthrightly homophobic and sexist of the Asian American male writers I have studied, it critiques U.S. White supremacy in an appealingly spirited manner. In my classroom experience, male Asian American students in particular have spoken passionately about Chin's role in raising their race consciousness and pride. As a result, I have often feared that, as much as Chin's gender politics need to be addressed, my doing so could take on the appearance of a racist silencing or dismissal. Today, however, I write with the conviction that the fear of critiquing things that we like or respect only reflects a naive belief that a cultural object can achieve a fully unproblematic status. In a world run through with so many forms of injustice, such a belief simply cannot be maintained. The value of an intersectional approach to reading the gender and race politics of Chin's writing is that it exposes that writing's problems without impugning the overall value of Chin's contribution to Asian American culture.

My understanding of intersectional politics in Asian American literature is due in large part to the work of Elaine Kim and King-Kok Cheung. Their intersectional critical practice has informed not only my understanding of Chin, but the direction of my entire project. In a 1990 article, Elaine Kim writes:

> In the peculiarly American tangle of race and gender hierarchies, the objectification of Asian Americans as permanent outsiders has been tightly plaited with our objectification as sexual deviants: Asian men have been coded as having no sexuality, while Asian women have nothing else…both exist to define the white man's virility and the white race's superiority.[1]

Kim's analysis exposes the poverty of a single-axis critical approach to the discriminatory mechanisms affecting Asian Americans. Anti-racist discourse cannot set aside gender concerns for a "pure" analysis of racial/ethnic subordination as long as White supremacist power "plaits" them together. Effective counterhegemonic Asian American political strategy must therefore have a multiple-axis construction: it must encompass—at least—race and gender concerns. Male Asian American critics also have been aware of this necessity. As early as 1972, in an article titled "Racist Love," Frank Chin and Jeffrey Paul Chan noted how racial stereotypes about Asian American men dovetail with sexual ones.[2] They argue persuasively that, different from the racist representations of Latino, African American and American Indian men as hyper-masculine, White imagination has constructed Asian American men as effeminized and passive. The difference between this powerful, amusing article and related work by Kim and others is that the anti-racist strategies advocated in "Racist Love," as well as later pieces by Chin and Chan, insist upon the "masculinization" of Asian American men through the revival of a heroic Chinese and Japanese tradition. As an alternative to the nodal points which structure a White discourse of Asian American maleness—"effeminacy," "passivity," "infantilism," "humility," etc.—Chin puts forward a discourse which he claims originates in a Chinese/Japanese warrior tradition. This conception of Asian American manhood contradicts the one constructed by White America, valorizing, as it does, traits traditionally marked as masculine.

Unfortunately, I would argue, the antagonisms which Chin's discourse creates are not, in the end, against subordinating White power. By privileging heroic terms such as bravery, strength, independence and honor, Chin creates a hegemonic bloc which, even if it does have Asian origins, sets itself up in a relationship of equivalence with the similarly structured discourse of White masculinity. Despite the fact that Chin conceives of his project as one which combats White supremacy, the identity-forming hegemonic bloc which arises from his alternative vision of Asian America is one between Asian American and White heterosexual men. Antagonisms therefore arise between Asian American men and women, and between male heterosexuals and homosexuals of all races.

King-Kok Cheung points out such dangers in Chin's politics in her 1990 article, "The Woman Warrior versus The Chinaman Pacific: Must a Chinese American Critic Choose between Feminism and Heroism?":

> If Chinese American men use the Asian heroic dispensation to promote male aggression, they may risk making themselves in the image of their oppressors—albeit under the guise of Asian panoply. Precisely because the racist treatment of Asians has taken the peculiar form of sexism—insofar as the indignities suffered by men of Chinese descent are analogous to those traditionally suffered by women—we must refrain from

seeking antifeminist solutions to racism. To do otherwise reinforces not only patriarchy but also white supremacy.[3]

Chin's strategy is gutted of much of its anti-racist power when it aligns itself with heterosexual White men, the group benefiting most from all types of oppression, including racial oppression, in the United States. There is, moreover, little reason to believe that the White male imagination will react to writings like Chin's by refiguring its stereotype of Asian American men in an effort to establish a relationship of full equivalence with them. The only thing Chin's politics ensures is that women and "effeminized" men in the Asian American community will be disaffected from him and his supporters, and White power will face a divided community.[4]

Cheung and Kim's critique of Chin is thorough yet respectful of his value as an artist, thinker and activist. I would like to extend their analysis and examine what I perceive as a trend in Asian American male writing. Chin's masculinist strategy to combat White supremacist hegemony, I will argue, is but an instance (admittedly an unusually clear one) in a tradition of such thought. To suggest that Chin is somehow an isolated or rare example of masculinist anti-racist Asian American writing misses the pervasiveness of this problem. I will argue that a number of the most widely read texts by Asian American male writers are masculinist/heterosexist in their understanding of U.S. racism and their strategizing for change.

Feminist critics have located the four writers (Chin, Chan, Wong and Inada) associated with the anthologies, *Aiiieeeee!*[5] and *The Big Aiiieeeee!*, as primary bearers of a masculinist Asian American critical bias. Sau-Ling Cynthia Wong, for example, singles them out, criticizing the gender "reverse essentialism—discernible in the *Aiiieeeee* (Chin et al.) group's blatant sexism and inadvertently betrayed self-contempt."[6] She adds, "The *Aiiieeeee* school dismisses the reality of sexism and gender politics for Chinese American women."[7] Paralleling Kim and Cheung, Wong argues that these male writers' error lies in regarding "gender and ethnicity as discrete," when, she writes, "in a society like that of the United States, ethnicity is, in some sense, always already gendered, and gender always already ethnicized."[8] Sexist bias, of course, does not originate with Chin and the others. It is part of global historical patriarchal tradition affecting writers, male and female, of all ethnicities. Given, however, the relatively powerful position the *Aiiieeeee!* editors have achieved, both as writers and advocates for other writers, it is important to thoroughly examine their work, the work they promote and the manner in which they promote that work.

One can, for example, identify powerful masculinist biases in the work of many of the writers Chin et al. put forward for canonization.[9] In their introduction to *Yardbird Reader #3*, Chin and Wong describe John Okada, the author of *No-No-Boy*, as Asian American literature's "greatest pioneer."[10] Elsewhere, Inada calls *No-No Boy* "one of the great works of our time" and claims that its protagonist, Ichiro, ""exemplifies the quest of Japanese America for its own self."[11] Given the power of Okada's novel and its undeservedly poor initial reception, Chin, Wong and Inada's praise is understandable and long overdue. Their assessment of Okada's work could nevertheless be enriched by a critique of the masculinist vision of the novel. Beneath the moving story of *No-No Boy*, John Okada articulates a strategy of empowerment for Asian American men through "masculinization" which is similar to Chin's.

Okada's novel demonstrates the literal ways in which institutionalized racism endangers the lives of people of color. He meticulously outlines the logic of oppression by looking at, among other things, racial/ethnic employment discrimination, the psychological effects of internment on Japanese Americans, the devaluation of Asian and other non-European cultures by the White-controlled U.S. media, and the general physical and verbal harassment of Post-WWII Japanese Americans. As much as these representations succeed, however, Okada's implicit strategy for resistance fares less well, due, at least in part, to its masculinist bias.[12]

Okada creates a world whose relentlessly Darwinian gender prescriptions, no less than, and in conjunction with, the racism he describes, determine which characters will survive. The discourse of masculinity which structures *No-No Boy* is so powerful that even a single transgression of any part of its coded demands can doom a character. My reading of *No-No Boy* attempts a double movement of disentangling the discourses of race and gender while at the same time understanding their inseparability in the text and the implications of their intersectionality. I will look, in particular, at the male Nisei characters in the novel and the way that their fates in a racist political system are influenced by their gender identification. Ultimately, I hope to suggest that, as a textual interpellating force, *No-No Boy* "recruits" Asian American readers as anti-racist subjects in a heterosexist, and thus limited, if not dangerous, manner.

The dominant informing discourse of Nisei masculinity coalesces around a set of tropes which signify both physiological and behavioral characteristics. Roughly speaking, this discourse insists that a Nisei man must not be small either in height or weight, must speak in a forceful voice, must strictly avoid "domestic" activities, must evince an active heterosexuality, and must prove himself in physical combat. Given that only the most masculinized Nisei men are alive at the end of the novel, Ichiro's movement from transgression to complete embodiment of this gender code takes on an aura of necessity. In other words, the text argues that Ichiro survives racism, in large part, because he is able to articulate himself as an ideal masculine subject.

One of the many qualifications I must add to my analysis is that the discursive demands on masculinity which I examine apply only to the Nisei characters in the novel. Their Issei fathers seemingly operate within a different gender system. They possess characteristics which would doom their Nisei sons. Ichiro's father, for instance, is described as "short," "gently spoken," "feeble," and "fearful," among other things. He also transgresses conventional gender rules by being the primary preparer of food in his family[13] and by allowing his son to beat him. At one point Ichiro goes so far as to declare that his father "should have been a woman."[14] In a less exaggerated, but similar way, Bob Kumasaka and Kenji Kanno's Issei fathers take up a gender identity antithetical to that demanded of their sons. The former is also small and speaks softly; the latter lives as a widower, cooking for his family. Due to the limited scope of this chapter, however, the very interesting opposition Okada lays out across generational lines cannot be examined at any length. It must suffice here to suggest that since the generational rupture in gender requirements corresponds to the rupture between the sons' and fathers' national identies, the links between masculinity and resistance to racism find a further overdetermination with the added consideration of immigration status.[15]

Several of Ichiro's fellow Nisei—Gary, Bob, Fred, and Kenji—stand as real victims of anti-Japanese racism, but the fullness of Okada's understanding of their racial situation will be missed without confronting the role gender plays in his critique. Not all the Japanese Americans in *No-No Boy* are destroyed by racism, not even all the Nisei men. One thing that links the (in some ways) heterogeneous destruction of certain Nisei men is their place in the discourse of masculinity structuring the novel. Each of these four men fails to embody the full range of masculine characteristics vital to Okada's post-WWII Japanese American young men. By identifying similarities in Okada's representations of these men, I hope to prove the existence of regularly distributed gender tropes, and thus discover, negatively, through the destruction of these men, the shape of the discursive formation of masculinity which privileges Ichiro's physique as well as his gender "choices."

Ichiro's friend, Gary, is alive at the end of the novel, but it is difficult not to understand him largely as a casualty of racism. Ichiro finds him working at the Christian Rehabilitation Center, an organization whose own manager describes as a place for "drunks, morons, incompetents, delinquents, the physically handicapped" (220). The psychological consequences of Gary's internment and imprisonment land him in a place for people constitutionally unfit for ordinary jobs.

Gary's victimization is most evident in the toll taken on his private life. Having "died," as he says, in the prison where he was sent for refusing to serve in the armed forces, he has forsaken almost all human contact, giving up his friends and family in exchange for "art." He tells Ichiro:

> I came home and said hello to the family and tried to talk to them, but there was nothing to talk about. I didn't stay. I found a room, next to the sky, a big, drafty attic atop a dilapidated mansion full of boarders

who mind their own business. Old friends are now strangers. I've no
one to talk to and no desire to talk, for I have nothing to say except
what comes out of my paint tubes and brushes. (224)

One might view Gary's commitment to art as a triumph were it not for the fact that his art consists of painting signs on the sides of the Center's trucks.

What complicates Gary's victimization is the fact that even as Okada makes clear the racist origin of Gary's problems, he simultaneously imputes to him a symbolic gender "failure." First, the narrator marks Gary's masculine identity as precarious, noting that he "wasn't tall," is "slender" and speaks "softly." In addition to these physical characteristics, his social isolation puts him out of contact with women, making it impossible for him to fulfill the demand of compulsory active heterosexuality placed on Nisei men. Ichiro's friend, Freddie, underscores the sexual perilousness of Gary's position by describing the Christian Reclamation Center as not only a place for "drunks and dead beats," but for those paradigms of failed heterosexuality: "homos" (203).

The other three Nisei men are victims in the largest sense: they are killed. While their deaths—by gunshot, car accident, and disease—differ in obvious ways, they are tied together by the racist practices of U.S. society during and after World War II. They are also linked, however, by the characters' disarticulation from the novel's discourse of proper masculinity. The "quietness" of Bob Kumasaka, for instance, is the first quality put forward about him by the narrator. A further suggestion of Bob's failure to meet masculine expectations immediately follows. The narrator reports that he "never played football...or appeared at dances," but "could talk for hours on end about chemistry and zoology and physics" (27). Perhaps most significant in this passage is the implicit refusal, by not "appearing at dances," to participate in sexual behaviors marked as masculine. While his friend Jun does not criticize Bob for this reason, he does assert the need for masculine heterosexual behavior:

Me and the other guys, all we talked about was drinking and girls and
stuff like that because it's important to talk about those things when
you make it back from the front on your own power. (29-30)

It is during one of these "talks" that Bob, thinking about "how he was going to medical school and become a doctor," instead of about "girls and stuff like that," is struck dead by a stray bullet. At this moment, the critique of racism implicit in Bob Kumasaka's battlefield death, fighting on the side of men who have put his own people into concentration camps, becomes entangled with a discourse of masculinity. It is as if the bullet which kills simultaneously acts as the symbolic bearer of racist violence and the avenger of gender transgression. In this way, Bob's failure to demonstrate active heterosexual desire, while linked in no literal way to his death, nevertheless reinforces the symbolic gender logic of the novel and insists on the connection between proper masculine behavior and survival in a racist world.

Another of *No-No Boy*'s Nisei men, Fred Akimoto, fails to negotiate the masculine exigencies of the novel in ways strikingly reminiscent of Bob. Fred's voice, though not soft, is nonetheless presented as reduced, robbed of power. The narrator describes him speaking "like a little kid" (235). Likewise, his heterosexuality, though evident in ways Bob's is not, is also undercut, characterized always in terms of failure. Although Fred is involved in a heterosexual relationship, he does not understand this relationship as a "success." Describing his lover, he says, "I'm the guy what used to be so damn particular about dames. She's nothing but a fat pig" (47). Forays outside of this relationship to validate himself sexually also meet with failure. When he and Ichiro seek out a prostitute, the pimp, Rabbit, contradicting reports that "'Any time you want a gal…Rabbit's the boy to see,'" says to them, "All my girls are booked" (238). Even the always fertile Rabbit is unable to facilitate Fred's heterosexuality. As if to reinforce this idea of Fred's emasculation, when Rabbit admires Fred's watch, Fred angrily shoots back, "So whattaya want me to do? Go to bed with it?" Rabbit replies, "You're small enough all right" (238). With these words, Fred's forestalled heterosexuality is linked up with another of *No-No Boy*'s emasculating tropes: physical smallness.

Fred is described as "small," as "a little man" and a "young boy"; he possesses "small shoulders"; he is called "that little bastard," "the little man," "Shorty"; and in a barfight, the narrator refers to him as an "undersized opponent." Even his death in an automobile accident underlines the diminutizing insistence of his characterization. An observer describes him as having been "just about cut in two" (249). It must also be noted that this accident takes place as a literal consequence of Fred's divergence from *No-No Boy*'s code of masculinity: he crashes his car in panicked retreat from a barfight.

Kenji Kanno, perhaps the most sympathetic character in *No-No Boy*, provides an even greater example of the final determinacy of the masculine gender prescriptions discussed in the three previous examples. Like Gary, Bob, and Fred, Kenji does not possess a "masculine" voice; he is "shy, unassuming Kenji," a "soft-spoken veteran." Like Fred, Kenji has a "slight figure." He describes himself as "a small guy with small wants." Moreover, like the other three men, he fails to meet the demand of active heterosexuality. Kenji hints that the war injury which cost him his leg also has rendered him impotent. For this reason, when he senses his friend Emi's need for sexual release he arranges for her to sleep with Ichiro: "I'm only half a man, Ichiro, and when my leg starts aching, even that half is no good" (89). Kenji's "castration" is symbolized by the creeping gangrenous loss of his leg. And when the gangrene actually takes Kenji's life, Okada raises the stakes of this symbolization to the highest level: emasculation becomes a death sentence.

A final point of gender transgression comes with Kenji's acceptance of traditionally female domestic occupations. Throughout the novel, Kenji nurtures those around him, matchmaking Emi and Ichiro with selfless concern. The morning after the tryst he arranges between the two, they awaken to find "Kenji getting breakfast ready. He looked up from the frying eggs and grinned sheepishly" (99). Okada writes that Emi "took over the stove," watching "sadly...as Kenji limped carefully to the table" (99-100). It is as though she understands the fatal consequences of as small a gender transgression as the preparation of food by a man. And, indeed, this morning she sees Kenji for the last time.

No-No Boy thus articulates the intersection of the secondary male Nisei characters' racial victimization and their transgression of a strict discourse of masculinity. The main narrative of *No-No Boy*, however, is the triumphant story of Ichiro's rearticulation of himself as an appropriately masculine American subject. From the beginning of the novel, in which he is in danger of relinquishing his claim to masculinity, to the end, when he has restructured his identity around the nodal points of the novel's dominant discourse of gender, Ichiro's development argues for the desirability, if not necessity, of male Nisei identification with a strict conception of masculinity.

Ichiro is lucky enough to enter life with a gender "advantage" over the victimized Nisei men because of his masculine build. His father admires "his son who was Japanese but who had been big enough for football and tall enough for basketball in high school" (7). He has also developed a powerful male voice which he employs even at the low point of his emasculation. In the novel, he yells, shrieks, shouts—even when he "mutters" it is done "viciously." Finally, although he eats and makes a mess many times in the novel, Ichiro never performs the domestic jobs which accommodate such activities. In all these ways, Ichiro's manhood is secure; it is rather in the struggles in the fields of sexuality and violence that Ichiro risks destruction. His eventual self-rearticulation in these areas ensures that Ichiro will not be another victim of White racism.

When the novel begins, these two crucial aspects of Ichiro's masculinity are in question. As for his heterosexuality, the first page of the novel finds Ichiro just released from prison and its attendant two-year enforced separation from women. This separation, however, has not heightened his sexual drive; Ichiro seems altogether devoid of heterosexual desire. Standing at a bus stop, he looks at "half a dozen women who failed to arouse him even after prolonged good behavior" (1). The absence of heterosexual interest is to be understood as a result of Ichiro's depressed alienation in White America. The novel, however, offers a history of Ichiro's sexual "failures" which lends a different significance to his opening impotence.

"This Thing Going With My Bride to Straighten Out in America" 23

In recollecting his first sexual encounter, Ichiro identifies himself in a passive role. He tells Kenji, "I remember the first time I laid a girl. She was a redhead in my history class. Knew her way around. I guess, actually, she laid me. I was scared" (72). This woman symbolically unmans him, "knowing her way around" where he doesn't, and "laying" him when it is his masculine duty to assert authority in sex. From his first sexual encounter, Ichiro is threatened with the loss of masculine sexual viability, so that years later, having been separated from women in prison, he emerges without heterosexual desire.[16]

When Ichiro discovers that Kenji and Emi have arranged a sexual liaison for him, he reacts with "anger" and is plunged into indecision about how to act:

> Ichiro sat and fumed, struggling to do the right thing and not knowing what it was. If Kenji had said another word or allowed even a tiny smile to rise to his lips, he would have snatched the keys and rushed out. (89)

The fact that Ichiro does nothing to seduce Emi undercuts the impending heterosexual act's aura of masculine agency, something he requires much more than sexual gratification. Even after he crawls into bed with Emi, Ichiro is unable to act:

> His body taut and uncomfortable, he lay stiffly and stared at the ceiling. He fought for something to say, some remark to start bridging the gap of starched sheet that stretched between them. (90)

Ichiro's unease is broken only when Emi takes his hand with her own "warm and friendly and relaxing" one.

Although Ichiro has resumed heterosexual activity, Okada still casts him as the sexually passive partner; after several pages of pillow talk, it is Emi who initiates their sexual encounter. The narrator emphasizes her power over Ichiro, rendering their intimacy as that between parent and child, with all its attendant power differentials: "Emi reached out her free hand and drew his face to her naked breast. Lost and bewildered like a child frightened, he sobbed quietly" (92).

The next morning, Emi is still in control of the sexual encounter of the night before. Dressed in men's clothing—"a pair of man's overall pants...and a heavy athletic sweater"—Emi, as the dominant participant in what has transpired the night before, sets the terms of its later interpretation. Interrupting his "hesitant" opening words, "I want you to know," Emi insists, "You mustn't...Talking will make it sound bad and unclean and it was not so" (93). Ichiro sees "the truth in her words," granting even epistemological authority to Emi. He leaves Emi's farm having made a small step—actual heterosexual performance—towards the masculine demands on his sexuality, but remains largely effeminized and, thus, in danger.

His second encounter with Emi is even less promising. After dinner, he tells her that although in time he will "surely love [her] very deeply," he must leave her since she is already married. Despite her tearful assurances that her husband will never return, Ichiro leaves, the last words of the chapter depicting him in sexual flight as he "runs out of the house."

Ichiro assumes a full masculine/heterosexual identity only in his final encounter with Emi. As the scene opens, she retains her position of dominance by arriving at Ichiro's house on her own initiative. She maintains her earlier position of assertiveness by initiating physical contact, putting a "hand over his" as they talk at the table. She announces her impending divorce, removing Ichiro's ostensible objection to pursuing a relationship. He still refuses, however, her naked plea to "Come and see me." Only when she has gotten up to go and, following a litany of her crushed hopes, has described her desires as "thoughts of a little girl," does Ichiro transform. It is as though only Emi's characterization of herself as a child can make Ichiro accept his responsibility and privilege as a man. After sexually dominating Ichiro, she opens perhaps the only space in which Ichiro can assume a position of dominance over her: she represents herself as a child. In immediate response to Emi's words, Ichiro says, "Let's go," and leads her off to a dancehall. With a virtually performative act of language, Ichiro breaks through his sexual malaise, instantaneously recovering his absent masculine heterosexuality. His relationship with Emi undergoes a radical transformation. Whereas before Emi took upon herself not only all sexual initiative, but all decision-making responsibilities, she is suddenly passive. She suggests that going dancing so soon after Ichiro's mother's funeral is inappropriate, but is overborn by Ichiro. Okada writes that she "seemed to want to protest further but said no more" (208). In the car Ichiro asks her where she wants to go and she replies, "Wherever you wish." At this point, Ichiro has stepped from among his fellow Nisei into an "appropriately" subordinating relationship towards women and a heterosexuality which will allow him to survive in the world of the No-No Boy.

All that remains for Ichiro is to prove himself capable of violent physicality. His internment and imprisonment leave him in a state of physical and emotional alienation and inertia, and since the novel links racial victimization to tropes of masculinity in the novel, Ichiro's political resistance only becomes effective when it proves itself capable of masculinely marked physical violence. If he can strike out with his body, if he fights oppression through the use of physical violence, he will be safe.

In the beginning of the novel, at the bus stop where Ichiro looks without desire at women, he runs into Eto, an old acquaintance of his, a veteran whose evident masculinity provides a stark contrast to his own ambiguous gender position. Eto's military dress suggests his barely latent violence: "the face had hardened, but the hair was still cropped. The fellow wore green, army-fatigue trousers and an Eisenhower jacket" (2). Eto calls Ichiro "no-no boy," says "Rotten bastard. Shit on you," and spits on him. Rather than resist or even resent this treatment, Ichiro symbolically acknowledges its justness. He bends before Eto's superior masculinity:

> The legs of his accuser were in front of him. God in a pair of green fatigues, U.S. Army style. They were the legs of the jury that had passed sentence upon him. Beseech me, they seemed to say, throw your arms about me and bury your head between my knees and seek pardon for your great sin. (4)

Only recently free of his debasing prison experience, Ichiro is in a psychological state of intense self doubt and cannot defend himself against humiliation at the hands of another man:

> The walls had closed in and were crushing all the unspoken words back down into his stomach. He shook his head once, not wanting to evade the eyes but finding it impossible to meet them. Out of his big weakness the little ones were branching, and the eyes he didn't have the courage to face were ever present. If it would have helped to gouge out his own eyes, he would have done so long ago. The hate-churned eyes with the stamp of unrelenting condemnation were his cross and he had driven the nails with his own hands. (3-4)

By asserting that he "had driven the nails with his own hand," the text implicates Ichiro in his own victimization, but simultaneously grants him an agency which he can redirect to resist further such humiliations. Hands that drive nails can also fight back. Ichiro must identify the masculine code of violent resistance and rearticulate himself according to its terms if he wishes to survive in the world to which he is returning.

His next fight goes little better, however. One night in a bar, a hypermasculine Nisei, significantly named "Bull," insults Ichiro. Although indignant "fury" "seethes uncontrollably" inside him, Ichiro cannot defend himself against Bull with the violence the situation requires. "Shame," writes Okada, "deprived him of the strength to release the turbulence" (75). Leaving the bar, he is subjected to further humiliation. Friends of his brother, Taro, another masculinized Nisei figure, attack him outside, and although they are only a "gang of weak hoodlums," they force Ichiro to the ground and attempt to strip him of his pants. The symbolic castration of this act comes close to being literalized when one of his attackers starts "to slip [a] knife blade under the leather belt" (79). Subject to racism-induced passivity, Ichiro not only is unable to protect himself from physical assault, he must rely on a disabled, literally weaker man to rescue him. Kenji intervenes, knocking away the attackers of Ichiro's manhood with his substitute phallus, a cane.

By having Bull and the other attackers single out Ichiro for persecution because of his refusal to serve in the army, Okada demonstrates effectively how racist hegemony diverts attention from the White origins of oppression by dividing communities of color. But from beneath this insight into the mechanics of racial domination, a call for stereotypical masculinity emerges. This scene suggests that survival in a racist world, far from a political abstraction, requires a concrete strategy of physical self-empowerment. Through his experiences and observations of the racial and gender rules of his world, Ichiro is, finally, in the last chapter of the novel, able to rearticulate himself in a manner strictly in accordance with the novel's operative discourse of masculinity.

In the final scene of *No-No Boy*, Ichiro attacks Bull in order to protect Freddie, and manages, in the course of the fight, to "gain the top position." From this height, Ichiro enters a state of overdetermined rage: his immediate enemy, Bull, simultaneously stands in for all the emasculating and racist forces in the novel, forces which have made him a No-No Boy and then persecuted him for being one, forces which have threatened to unman him to the point of death. Okada writes: "urged by a need to fight this thing which no amount of fighting would ever destroy, Ichiro raised his fist and drove it down" (247). His physical defeat of Bull is complete. Bull, until this moment the epitome of masculinity in the novel, is reduced by Ichiro's now superior manhood to a person crying, "not like a man in grief or a soldier in pain, but like a baby in loud, gasping, beseeching howls" (250). This fight marks Ichiro's emergence into the promise of full-blown masculine identity. As he walks away from this violent victory, Ichiro seems to emerge from racial subordination as well:

> A glimmer of hope—was that it? It was there, someplace. He couldn't see it to put it into words, but the feeling was pretty strong.
> He walked along, thinking, searching, thinking and probing, and, in the darkness of the alley of the community that was a tiny bit of America, he chased that faint and elusive insinuation of promise as it continued to take shape in mind and in heart. (251)

With these, the last words of the novel, Ichiro's crisis of masculinity is not only resolved, but is finally and inextricably tied to his position as a racial Other in America. A victor in the final test of his masculinity, Ichiro, moving in his "tiny bit of America," is at last within reach of a full American identity.

Okada's strategy in *No-No Boy* is similar to Chin's in suggesting that the racial subordination of Asian American men can be countered by masculinization. As in Chin's discourse, the nodal points of the discursive formation of masculinity in Okada's text articulate positive Asian American male characters antithetically to the ways in which they have been stereotypically understood and represented in the cultural productions of White America. The sexual, domestic, build, and violence components of Okada's discourse react against White stereotypes about Asian American men which attempt to represent them as "essentially feminine in character." Soft-spokenness and physical powerlessness evoke the marginalization of

Asian American political concerns and the denial of self-representation through an Asian American voice. But one must interrogate a politics which fights stereotypes through identification with the same cultural valuations which lend those stereotypes a racist/sexist valence.

While Okada's desire for change is undeniable, the structuring of his racial politics around a mascunlinist understanding of gender leads him in politically dangerous directions. By valorizing, in terms of mere survival, only ultra-masculine Nisei men, Okada denies himself relevance for the larger Japanese American community to which he meant to address himself. The hetero/sexism of his conception of masculinity fails to speak to the concerns of women and gay men in his community. The specificity of his anti-racist strategy and its partial antagonism to the interests of many others in the Japanese American community not only preclude it from speaking for those others, but may actively work to subordinate them.

Some negative consequences of Ichiro's masculinization become immediately apparent. A wall of silence, for example, is erected between him and Emi. After Ichiro's sexual "breakthrough," Okada writes, "They didn't say much either in the car or after they found a sizable roadhouse and started dancing" (209). Once Ichiro has assumed his manhood, there seems to be nothing to say to women. Their silence becomes meaningful and comprehensible. Their bliss is premised on an absence of need for, or else prohibition against, conversation. They dance happily, smiling "at each other, for there really was nothing to be said" (210). Ichiro's return to a "proper" relation to women thus reinstates a dynamic in which spheres of gender experience are separate and autonomous. This simple reassertion of unbridgeable sexual difference, however, in no way benefits women, since this dichotomy is always already marked not as a relationship of simple difference, but as one of women's subordination, nor does it benefit men who desire intimacy with women. Emi's final submissiveness and the death of Ichiro's improperly masculinized Ma further limit the appeal to women of Okada's sexual politics.

Ultimately, Japanese Americans whose gender/sexuality in any way diverges from Okada's rigidly heterosexist model, can hardly take comfort in a politics which argues that their obliteration is somehow natural or inevitable. Okada's presentation of the almost Darwinian exigiencies of masculinity not only ignores the experiences of women and lesbians and gays of color, it buttresses the sexism and homophobia to which they are subject. I am not suggesting, however, that Okada's text should therefore not be read. On the contrary, as one of the inaugural works of Japanese American fiction, it must be confronted. But this confrontation must be two-fold in character: even as it acknowledges the novel as a insightful expression of the experience of a marginalized racial Other in the U.S., it must work to disentangle the latent subordinating discourse of gender which undermines its ability to speak for the Japanese American community.

As I noted above, Chin's appreciation of Okada is shared by, among others, Chin's coeditor, Shawn Wong. Wong's 1979 *Homebase*, only the second novel (after *Eat a Bowl of Tea*) published in the United States by a Chinese American man, is, like Chin's and Okada's novels, inspiring in its resistant stance toward White supremacist domination. But like these other writers, Wong employs a regrettably masculinist strategy for challenging White power. He reflects, perhaps in less obvious ways, patriarchal/heterosexist biases in his apprehension of U.S. racism and in his strategies for resistance. His novel, *Homebase*, has been widely praised both for its artistry and its meditation on Asian American identity. Most critics who discuss *Homebase*'s identity politics, however, neglect to examine the masculinist orientation of the novel and the implications of that orientation.

Oggie Kim's review in *Bridge*, for example, contrasts Wong's novel favorably to Maxine Hong Kingston's *China Men*, writing, "Where *China Men* lacks central protagonists, Rainsford in *Homebase* is identifiable and elicits both interest and empathy."[17] This interest and empathy, in Kim's estimation, derive from what she perceives as the universality of the text:

> By using his personal experiences, Wong touches a universal note. Almost everyone at one time or another has felt some disaffection and crisis of identity. Especially for Asians and other minorities there is often a tension and anxiety resulting from not having much affection for the ethnic home, and yet also feeling like a stranger in the country of citizenship. (28)

But while Kim criticizes the gender politics of Kingston's text (arguing, for example that "Kingston through her fable inculcates the male fear of women as castrators, emasculators of men" (28)), she disregards the gender politics of Wong's text, as well her as her own. Her loose use of gender pronouns emerges, for example, in her praise for *Homebase*'s "resolution at the end: that each man must come to terms with his own identity" (28). She furthermore asserts that the protagonist's "selection of a blond, blue-eyed child-women connotes a universal fantasy of having a young, vacuous nymphet to control and manipulate" (28). Needless to say, this fantasy is not shared by all.

In his article, "Ethnicity and the Arts of Memory," prominent anthropologist Michael M.J. Fischer argues that autobiographical writings "can perhaps serve as key forms for explorations of pluralist, post-industrial, late twentieth-century society.[18] Fischer puts forth *Homebase* as a model of such writing and notes Wong's success in claiming U.S. identity by "mark[ing] and appropriat[ing] the land" through the psychoanalytic process of dream-work. In the limited space of his discussion of the novel, however, Fischer does not consider the limitations deriving from the fact that *Homebase*'s protagonist Rainsford's "territorial" assumption of identity is articulated in terms of patrilineal inheritance from his U.S. father and grandfathers. The limits of such political dream-work are evident both for women and for more recent Chinese American immigrants.

Chinese American writer Diana Chang, in her review of *Homebase*, implicitly accepts the masculinist bias in Wong's vision of American identity as well. Near the end of her piece, she describes a letter from Rainsford:

> He himself writes to his father: "A woman I love, Father, told me that identity is a word full of the home. Identity is a word that whispers, not whispers, but gets you to say, 'ever yours'" (p.31). He is, always will be, theirs, and they his; he is also America's.[19]

Chang's pronouns, "they" and "theirs," by which she refers to the narrator's parents, misrepresents the fact that the narrator's words address his dead father alone. In this letter, Rainsford refers to his mother only by the third person form, "my mother," as opposed to the direct address he uses for his father. Thus, the association of "home" with being "ever yours" becomes strictly a paternal identification, not a broader parental one. Later in the letter he reiterates, "Dear Father, I say, I write, I sing, I give you my love, this is a letter whispering those words, 'ever, ever yours'" (27).

Of all the commentary on Wong's novel, perhaps most surprising in this context is Elaine Kim's discussion of *Homebase* in her groundbreaking study, *Asian American Literature: An Introduction to the Writings and Their Social Context*. As sensitive as she is to the gender bias in Frank Chin's work, Kim has nothing to say about Wong's gender politics. She favorably contrasts Wong to Chin, writing, "Chin's gloom and pessimism is counterbalanced in Shawn Hsu Wong's short novel, *Homebase*."[20] For Kim, as for Fischer and Chang, much of the value of Wong's work lies in its territorial strategy for establishing Chinese American identity:

> *Homebase* is about a Chinese American's journey to search for and claim roots in American soil. The book emerges as a triumphant reaffirmation of the Chinese American heritage and ends with a reconciliation between father and son, who are linked by their American roots. (194)

In celebrating the ethnic/national identity politics of Wong's work, Kim glosses over the gendering of that politics, even as she identifies its basis in the "reconciliation between father and son." Kim seems to reaffirm the gendered, if not patriarchal character of the novel's politics of national identity near the end of her comments on Wong: "By claiming America as his own and by reaffirming the love that connects his life to the lives of his father and forefathers, Rainsford can affirm his American identity" (196).[21]

Kim is correct that *Homebase*'s strategy for establishing "American" identity involves cross-generational male bonding, but she does not pursue the problematics of such a strategy. Although Wong's novel does not polemicize in the manner of Frank Chin's nonfiction, it nevertheless articulates a discourse of Asian American identity which is exclusively masculine. As with Chin's description of Asian American identity, the characteristics which allow for the becoming-American of Rainsford are stereotypically masculine, if not "heroic."

It is clear from the beginning of the novel, for example, that Rainsford has been brought up in a manner to render him as masculine as possible. At the level of personal style, he recalls the "Superman shirt," "sailor's hat" and "replica of a long-barreled Colt" which his parents confer on him.[22] His father encourages Rainsford's masculine identification by involving him in traditionally masculine interests:

> Until my father died he had brought me up on all the childhood heroes. He indulged me in my fantasies and fascinations with planes, cars, cowboys, comic book heroes, and trains. He took me down to Berkeley's Aquatic Park two or three times a week to watch the trains pull in to the factories bordering the lake. We sat in the car parked under a tree watching the trains for hours at a time. (36)

Throughout, Rainsford emphasizes the active character of his father's role in this socialization: "When my father took pictures of those planes for me, and when we waited hours for those trains to pass by Aquatic Park, he encouraged my enthusiasm and imagination" (38). Rainsford's father strengthens this masculine socialization through role modeling and role playing: to Rainsford, it is "my father, the track star" (26); they act out jet fighter pilots together; in Guam, his father plays "General of the Beach" or floats Rainsford "out on a raft, swimming like Tarzan, with the raft's rope in his teeth" (62).

Once he is orphaned, Rainsford adopts his nearest male relative as a role model replacement, stating, "I became the man my uncle was. I picked up his habits. I dressed like him" (44). More curious than the masculinizing influence of his male relatives, however, is the role his mother plays in Rainsford's gender socialization. He reports:

> it was my mother that controlled my growing until she too died eight years after my father's death. Not a startling revelation except when I saw her burial and I discovered that she had shaped the style of my manhood in accordance with her own competitive and ambitious self. I grew up watching my mother's face for direction, the movements of her body. (32)

Rainsford gives humorous examples of his mother's masculinizing influence[23]:

> "Shake my hand," my mother said...
> "Shake it again." I shook. "Harder." I shook harder. "Harder." I shook her hand as firmly as I could. "Now," she said, "whenever you are introduced to another man, remember to shake his hand as firmly as you can. End of lesson." (43-4)

Later in life Rainsford realizes, however, that his mother's active gendering of him arose not solely "in accordance with her own competitive and ambitious self," but also from her need to connect him with his dead father:

> when he died, my mother knew she had to tell me about his youth and the lives of my grandfathers as he had told her...She had to make me more than just her husband's son, more than understanding his sensibility, but rather make me realize it on my own and sometime in my life say simply that "I am the son of my father." (38)

His mother's success in this endeavor is confirmed at the scene of her death:

> she saw that I was now like my father, the track star, the basketball and ice hockey player, and whether I had realized it then or not did not matter to her, she had succeeded in forming me into her notion of manly style, and in her eyes I had become simply her husband's son. (36)

Becoming "simply" a man's son must, of course, be interrogated from a feminist context. Casting his mother as little more than a vehicle for connecting a son with his absent father is demeaning to her[24] such a reduction articulates a vision of binary gender difference grounded on unequal power distribution—the cornerstone of sexism.[25] What is immediately at issue in this chapter, however, is Rainsford's use of naturalizing rhetoric in his characterization of his awakening manhood.

Rainsford, after revealing his parents' active role in creating his sense of gender, claims that he realizes "on his own" his father's importance in his life, exemplifying the Althusserian process of interpellation. Even as Rainsford details his parents' gendering of him as a man, he makes a claim for an autonomously produced masculine identity. After describing the masculine clothes they dress him in and the masculine recreation into which his father draws him as a small child, Rainsford denies any paternal social control:

> He never imposed his ego on me to try and make me into something, his son, an educated man, a thrifty person, anything. He simply provided for me and assumed the responsibility of a parent. (42)

Rainsford's contradictory assertions starkly reveal the power of the interpellating process. The naturalizing character of ideological interpellation is so strong that he can claim as native or innate the masculine identity and paternal identification which he knows his father and mother have bestowed upon him.[26] As a result, Rainsford can make gender reifying statements such as: "When a son takes a risk of love, he naturally loves his father. He commits himself to his father" (6).[27] In perhaps the most arresting passage in a generally powerful text, Rainsford even uses erotic language to describe the intensity of his love for his father:

> Only in the first days after my father's death did I cry silently into my pillow, my lover, my hero gone, his name whispered on my lips as I cried; then one day I stopped crying for him, resolved to make my life like his; it gave me strength. (39-40)

I must stress that it is not my position that Rainsford does not "really" feel for his father or that his identification with him is not as strong as he claims. On the contrary, it is the power and "authentic" character of his love that not only makes it profound, but allows that love to overdetermine other identity categories, such as nationality. Gender, to be sure, does not take ideological precedence over national or racial identity, but the gender system exerts itself so strongly on Rainsford that it influences how he will work against racial subordination and toward full "American" identity.

Historically, the restricted economic incentives for and exclusionary laws against Chinese immigration created a disproportionate number of Chinese men in the United States.[28] As such, male Chinese Americans were generally those most immediately and obviously affected by anti-Chinese racism in the United States. Wong's poetic rendering of the devastating impact of inhuman labor practices and racist laws is, I believe, the most powerful aspect of *Homebase*. As part of his resistance to White subordination, Rainsford's identification with his forefathers therefore "makes sense." Unfortunately, as part of a discourse put into circulation in, for example, literature courses, Wong's novel closes off many of the avenues of counterhegemonic discursive strategy it attempts to open.

One danger the novel flirts with is the either/or logic of a concept Asian American cultural critics have designated as the "dual personality." Even Wong, as part of the *Aiiieeeee!* editorial group, calls attention to the fallacy of insisting on an inescapable split in Asian Americans between their "Asianness" and "Americanness."[29] Strangely, *Homebase* implicitly accepts a dichotomizing conceptualization of Asian American life through the negation of much of Rainsford's Chinese cultural heritage.

Although Rainsford's mother is a Chinese immigrant, "China" seems hardly to figure in his life; one could argue that Chinese cultural influence scarcely appears in the novel. To a certain degree, this is understandable, given that Rainsford grows up in the United States. It is curious, even troubling, however, that Rainsford's mother seems to transmit very little of what she must know of Chinese life to Rainsford, so eager is she to make him into an American man in the image of his father.

Rainsford's father's lack of Chinese identification is more understandable; his whole life as a U.S. citizen naturally renders his Chinese cultural ties and knowledge less strong or urgent. I wish, however, to critique the gendered structure of his father's thinking about national/racial identity. First of all, Rainsford's father displays a gender-inflected anti-Chinese bias. Recalling his parents' first meeting, Rainsford writes that his father felt:

> His life had been the opposite of hers, and the realm of his history and tradition did not resemble hers in any way...he dismissed her with his own form of racial arrogance...he noticed her that day simply because she was the same color as he and she was good-looking. (7)

Although her "color" draws the father's attention, her national Chinese background is, if anything, an obstacle to their relationship, for "young Chinese girls from China annoyed him" (8). *Homebase* contextualizes the father's discomfort with "Chinese girls" by revealing the impoverished, single sex conditions under which Chinese immigrant men lived.[30] But while the hardship of their lives was created by the economic exploitation of and racist U.S. laws against Chinese immigrant men, Rainsford's male ancestors apparently direct some of their resentment toward female images. A gendered symbol of China, for example, once comes to Rainsford's father in a dream:

> "Are you afraid of dying with me?" she asked, drawing his hand to her stomach, putting her moist mouth in his ear, making him deaf, his throat ached for the moist moss of trees.
> "Yes," he answered, knowing she was the nightmare that made China the bitterness of his grandfather's and father's life. (4)

Rainsford's male ancestors sublimate the anger and frustration they might reasonably direct toward "America" and its male bearers of authority instead into bitterness toward Chinese women they cannot have.

This bias seems to be another part of Rainsford's patrilineal heritage. Rainsford's adoption of his father's mode of thinking results in a sort of doubled identity binary. By linking his father's masculinity with his U.S. nationality and his mother's femininity with her status as a Chinese immigrant, he arbitrarily constructs an identity bloc linking gender and ethnicity in a doubly exclusionary way. Rainsford's acceptance of binary sexual division prohibits him from "choosing" anything other than a absolute masculine identification with his father; and since his father defines himself equally strictly as "American," Rainsford finds himself in absolute national, as well as gender, solidarity with his patrilineal ancestors. Put otherwise, the fact that his male ancestors lived in the United States, as opposed to his Chinese matrilineal ancestors, and that he has an oppositional notion of male/female identity, patriarchy and nationalistic pride dictate the "choice" of an "American" masculine identity.

Wong's story thus becomes one of mutually reinforcing, exclusionary notions of gender and national identity. The bitter legacy of Chinese immigration to the United States, with its isolation of Chinese American men, and Rainsford's particular gendered/nationalized upbringing frame a masculinist (if not somewhat anti-Chinese) vision of Chinese American life, and we must ask whether or not this is a vision of Asian America which creates solidarity, or one which fractures Chinese Americans, as well as other Asian Americans, across gender, national, or immigration status lines. The novel interrogates the value of this type of interpellation on Rainsford himself.

Much of the novel is taken up with the difficulty Rainsford faces as a successfully interpellated masculine subject. Rainsford reports:

> at fifteen I am violent, arrogant because I know what I want out of my life. I want to pursue life, I want life to be difficult for me. I want to test myself. I want to feel like I'm being chased on the road at night. (79)

As a result of his competitiveness, engendered by his father and mother, Rainsford's high school life includes "no dates, no dances, just swimming miles and miles and playing water polo" (34). Even as an adult, Rainsford's masculine competitiveness and sense of isolation lend his outlook an almost nihilistic valence:

> Had I climbed only one mountain in my life, I might have taken some pride in that as an accomplishment. It is an exercise of faith, of the heart, and once you've achieved that goal you have nothing to work for; it is a kind of disappointment to meet that goal. I do not consider death simply as tragedy, but rather the affirmation of life. (67)

Finally, and perhaps most troubling in all of *Homebase* is the adult Rainsford's symbolic struggle to free himself of his desire for a phantasmic fifteen year-old blonde bride. His interaction with her, which takes up much of the fourth chapter, revolves around the conflict between his desire for her and the anti-Asian racism she embodies

> She was a dream girl, a patronizing blond-haired girl of fifteen. And in the dream about me I'm hiking with her alone, making up for those restless years, the lonely years of my grandfathers. (64)

He thus rationalizes his fantasy of her as a kind of redress for the injustices committed against his forefathers. He describes her as his "whole responsibility to America. She is America" (66).

Against this young White woman, Rainsford counterposes a Chinese American woman whom he "loved," but who, he writes, "is only the myth of the perfect day until I do get back to her home, she is the summit I must turn to in the end" (68). While the idealization of the Chinese American woman may seem a "positive" alternative to Rainsford's unhealthy fascination with the White girl, the former does little to ameliorate the gender limitations of *Homebase*. As Patricia A. Sakurai notes in her article, "The Politics of Possession: Negotiating Identities in *American in Disguise*, *Homebase*, and *Farewell to Manzanar*," the Chinese American woman's role is "a static one, her character synonymous with the identity she supposedly represents; she is locked in time, fixed in and defined through her relationship with Rainsford."[31] The evident dependency of *Homebase*'s female characters can, Sakurai suggests, ultimately subvert the anti-racist thrust of the novel:

> by continuing to rely on a sign system that privileges men as actors and prescribes the passive role of women as objects of desire, by continuing to reinforce a compulsory heterosexuality and fixed categories of race, class, and gender to produce meaning, certain heterosexual variations of/reactions to the dominant version of the politics of possession (such as the rejection of the white female body, or the rejection or seeking out of the Asian American female body), despite their "liberating" effects in some regards, ultimately risk upholding the same problematic signifying practice and discursive politics as the very paradigm they set out to challenge.[32]

At the novel's end, Rainsford's return to the Chinese American woman is still deferred: "it will be some time before I get up there. I've got this thing going with my bride to straighten out America" (68). So while Wong suggests, through his struggle with his blonde child bride, the pathology of White supremacy, he offers no strategy for challenging it. By premising "straightening out America" on working through desire for (young) White women, Wong not only sets for himself a goal he cannot be assured of accomplishing, he articulates a (heterosexual male) strategy of resistance to racial subordination which is largely irrelevant to the general struggle of Asian Americans.

Homebase, like Okada's *No-No Boy*, is a valuable contribution to the history of literature representing Asian American experience. But Wong's novel, while aware of the oppressive history and character of White domination in the United States, stymies its own ability to break free of subordination, in large part, due to its articulation of anti-racist discourse with conservative conceptions of gender.

What I've said about these texts, it must be repeated, is aimed at finding ways to teach them and disseminate their critique of U.S. White supremacy without endorsing the problematic elements, particularly with regard to gender and sexuality, which they commonly possess. In some ways, it is "easier," perhaps even more pleasant teaching texts which seem already less problematic, which put forward progressive positions on race/nationality as well gender/sexuality. This ease and pleasantness no doubt partly account for the popularity of the work of Maxine Hong Kingston and Amy Tan, and rising stars such as Gish Jen, Cynthia Kadohata, Jessica Hagedorn and Fae Myenne Eng. But as we continue to teach canonized writers like Okada, Wong, and others, and if we commit ourselves to the truly pluralist goal of listening to contemporary Asian American male voices as well, it behooves us to explore strategies for untangling the discourses intersecting these works. We don't have to fear sexism, homophobia, even White supremacy in the texts we study; we, and our students, are smart and committed enough to find our way through.

Notes

1. Elaine Kim, "'Such Opposite Creatures': Men and Women in Asian American Literature," *Michigan Quarterly Review* 29.1 (Winter, 1990): 69.
2. Jeffrey Paul Chan and Frank Chin, "Racist Love," in *Seeing Through Shuck*, ed. Richard Kostelanetz (New York: Ballantine, 1972).
3. King-Kok Cheung, "The Woman Warrior versus The Chinaman Pacific: Must a Chinese American Critic Choose between Feminism and Heroism?," *Conflicts in Feminism*, ed. Marianne Hirsch and Evelyn Fox Keller (New York: Routledge, 1990), 244.
4. One strategy of Chin's politics, for example, has been his labeling of non-"heroic" Asian American writers as "white racist." Because the discursive formation for Asian American identity Chin puts forward is intersectionally structured around Asian racial and masculine gender terms, and because this formation works through a logic of exclusion, the paradoxical result of Chin's strategy is that writers whose gender politics diverge from his own fall into the Otherness of White power. His insistence on a revived heroic tradition as the only viable Asian American racial politics compels him to dismiss the contributions of many women and "gay-friendly" writers in his community. In the introduction to *The Big Aiiieeeee!*, an anthology of Asian American literature, Chin and Chan, along with Lawson Fusao Inada and Shawn Wong, dismiss the work of Jade Snow Wong, Virginia Lee, Betty Lee Sung, Maxine Hong Kingston, Amy Tan, and David Henry Hwang as "products of white racist imagination" ((New York: Meridian, 1991), xii). Maxine Hong Kingston has come under particularly harsh charges of racism by Chin.
5. Jeffrey Paul Chan et al., eds., *Aiiieeeee!: An Anthology of Asian American Writers* (New York: Mentor, 1974).
6. Sau-ling Cynthia Wong, "Ethnicizing Gender: An Exploration of Sexuality as Sign in Chinese Immigrant Literature," in *Reading the Literatures of Asian America*, eds. Shirley Geok-lin Lim and Amy Ling (Philadelphia: Temple University Press, 1992), 125-6.
7. Ibid., 126.
8. Ibid., 126.
9. To take one example, Chin and the other editors of *The Big Aiiieeeee!* describe Louis Chu's 1961 novel, *Eat a Bowl of Tea*, as one of only four Chinese American literary works which does not "suck off the white Christian fantasy of the Chinese as a Shangri-La people" (xii). In "Facing the Incurable: Patriarchy in *Eat a Bowl of Tea*," however, Ruth Y. Hsiao examines the persistence of sexist bias in the novel, even as Chu attempts to critique the sexism of the Chinatown bachelor community he depicts (in *Reading the Literatures of Asian America*, 151-62).
10. Frank Chin and Shawn Hsu Wong, "Introduction to *Yardbird Reader #3*," *Yardbird Reader #3* (Berkeley: Yardbird Publishing, 1974).

11. Lawson Fusao Inada, "Of Place and Displacement: The Range of Japanese-American Literature," in *Three American Literatures: Essays in Chicano, Native American, and Asian American Literature for Teachers of American Literature*, ed. Houston A. Baker, Jr. (New York: MLA, 1982), 261, 263.
12. Gayle K. Fujita Sato imputes another, specifically racial, failing to Okada's novel. She argues that "Okada 'resolves' his character's identity crisis through a binary opposition valuing '(white) American' over 'Japanese'"(256). As a result:
    No-No Boy reflects the negative legacy of "dual identity," a conceptualization of "Asian American" which divides "Asian" and "American" into separate spheres of existence...Although the self-destructive potential of "dual identity" is fully elaborated in Ichiro Yamada's struggle, the same binary opposition ultimately defines his "redemptive" journey. No-No Boy attempts to affirm "Japanese American" through a character who rejects everything "Japanese." ("Momotaro's Exile: John Okada's No-No Boy," in Reading the Literatures of Asian America), 239.
13. King-Kok Cheung has made me aware that it is not unusual (it may in fact be common) for Nisei men to cook. Such an observation, however, does not substantially alter my analysis, since my purpose is not to evaluate the accuracy of *No-No Boy*'s representation of Nisei men; I intend, rather, to examine the way in which this representation hails subjects and thus opens up and closes off various Asian American anti-racist strategic possibilities. Indeed, Okada's representation of Nisei male cooking may be a part of the systematic adoption of White patriarchal norms which Sato criticizes above.
14. John Okada, *No-No Boy* (Seattle: University of Washington Press, 1976), 113. Further references are cited in the text.
15. Fujita Sato's article notes differences between the novel's Issei fathers' national identification. In her reading of the novel Ichiro's father's "failure" is connected to his retention of "Japanese" qualities, as opposed to Kenji Kanno's father's more successful "Americanized" identity ("Momotaro's Exile," 247-8).
16. That his first, and emasculating, sexual experience is with a White woman merits some consideration. Although Okada does not pursue this racialized moment further, a suggestion nevertheless remains that female sexual control over Ichiro is related to his subordination by White power. His assumption of sexual agency and dominance comes only with a Japanese American woman.
17. Oggie Kim, "Will the Ideal Role Model Please Stand Up?," *Bridge* 8.2 (1982): 27.
18. Michael M.J. Fischer, "Ethnicity and the Post-Modern Arts of Memory," in *Writing Culture: The Poetics and Politics of Ethnography*, eds. James Clifford and George E. Marcus (Berkeley: University of California Press, 1986), 195.
19. Diana Chang, review of *Homebase*, *Amerasia Journal* 8.1 (1981): 139. Chang makes clear her reluctance to critique Wong's novel in a statement early in the

review: "*Homebase* is not a book to be examined. It's one to be vulnerable to" (137).
20. Elaine Kim, *Asian American Literature: An Introduction to the Writings and Their Social Context* (Philadelphia: Temple University Press, 1982), 194.
21. Kim's later essay, discussed above, does criticize Wong's novel as a participant in Asian American men's writings' tendency to represent women "only in relation to men, often as voiceless obstacles to or objects of their search for America"("'Such Opposite Creatures,'" 73).
22. Shawn Wong, *Homebase* (New York: Plume, 1979), 11. Further references are cited in the text.
23. In one evocative scene with his mother, Rainsford's heterosexuality is shown to be, at least in some part, the product of socialization, here, via the movies:
This was the mother I wanted to kiss like the movie stars when I was a little boy after seeing those movies of the stars grabbing each other, smearing lipstick, mussing up each other's hair, and gasping for breath. "Kiss me like in the movies, Mom...Close your eyes," I said. She closed her eyes. We kissed. In the dark. My room. "Goodbye," I said from the throat. (43)
24. Rainsford addresses his imaginary grandfather in a way that erases several generations of his female patrilineal ancestors: "you found a woman who fathered my father and he fathered me" (52).
25. Many of the qualities Rainsford affirms in her are precisely those that set her apart, in his eyes, from other women: "In raising me she was unlike most mothers, who used self-pity to stir their sons into some kind of responsible action. I was like her" (58).
26. The possibility of gender "failure" implicit in Rainsford's fear that he will not grow into a proper man argues against the inevitability of masculine gender identification. He addresses this fear to his father: "At fifteen, when my mother died, I thought my terror would increase with age. The terror that I would not be like you, the terror that I would never admit where my home stood rooted" (26-7).
27. Immediately before this statement Rainsford eschews a naturalizing explanation of son/father love for another based on power:
It is hard to really love your father. It is easy to respect him. When you are the same age, or even when you grow older than your father, like growing taller than him, your love changes to honor because yourself would like to be honored. (5-6)
It is doubtful Rainsford is using the generalizing "you" form in a gender inclusive manner.
28. In her study, *Asian Americans: An Interpretive History* (Boston: Twayne Publishing, 1991), Sucheng Chan notes:
During the three decades of unrestricted Chinese immigration, only about 9,000 Chinese women arrived in the continental United States. Throughout the latter half of the nineteenth century, according to

my analysis of population census records, no more than 5,000 Chinese women were found on the entire U.S. mainland at any one time. (104-5)

29. *Aiiieeeee!*, xvi.
30. Surprisingly, Rainsford undercuts the pathos of at least one of his ancestors' life without women by suggesting that he chose not to bring his wife to the United States:

    Great-Grandfather's wife was a delicate, yet a strong and energetic lady, insisting in her letters to Great-Grandfather to let her come and join him...yet he resisted her pleas, telling her that life was too dangerous for a woman. (12)

31. *Critical Mass: A Journal of Asian American Cultural Criticism* 1.1 (Fall 1993): 46.
32. Ibid., 48.

CHAPTER THREE

Hegemony and the Broad Celebration of Charles Johnson

Black feminism has reoriented the study of African American fiction by emphasizing the interconnections between gendered and raced identities. Valerie Smith ends her 1989 article, "Gender and Afro-Americanist Literary Theory and Criticism," with the following summation:

> As Afro-Americanist discourse has exposed the absences in the work of mainstream critics, questions of gender have forced the Afro-Americanist tradition to be increasingly self-evaluative and self-critical. Not at all diversionary, these explorations rather complicate the field, for they enable considerations of the various ways in which people of color, male and female alike, experience the conditions of oppression. Indeed, further elaborations upon the relationship between gender, race, and class, hold great promise for enriching the discipline. Textually grounded future work needs to be done, for instance, on the way constructions of masculinity affect the experience of race, and the way that connection is represented in literature.[1]

Smith's closing call for work on Black masculinity echoes similar calls by other Black feminists.

In her article, "Reflections on Race and Sex," bell hooks insists on:

> a space within feminist movement for the production, dissemination, and discussion of diverse ideas and perspectives. This includes focusing on black male thinkers and writers. I can understand the dissident black male voices who indict feminist thinkers for condemning their work without giving it serious critical appraisal, without seeking to understand where they are coming from.[2]

Similarly, in her essay, "Some Implications of Womanist Theory," Sherley Anne Williams notes:

> Having confronted what black men have said about us, it is now time for black feminist critics to confront black male writers with what they have said about themselves. What is needed is a thoroughgoing examination of male images in the works of black male writers.[3]

Since it issues from my experience as a White man, the following argument cannot present itself as a literal response to William's call, but it nevertheless grows out of a commitment to understanding the self-representations of African American men living in White supremacist, patriarchal culture. My intervention in the discourse about African American literature examines how, in the writings of Charles Johnson, racial and gender identity formations intersect and inform each other.

I have chosen Johnson in part because of the increased critical attention given to his work since he received the National Book Award in 1991 for *Middle Passage*—the first novel by an African American man to win the prize since Ralph Ellison's *Invisible Man*. I also have chosen to look at Charles Johnson because, while he clearly possesses an original and virtuosic creativity, he also puts forward a vision of race and gender which I believe to be deeply problematic. I must emphasize that the gender and race politics of Johnson's fiction are no more troubling than those of equally or more famous contemporary White male writers (Mailer, Pynchon, DeLillo, to name a few). In the context of contemporary Black male literary production, however, his accolades from the White-dominated media and academy should be interrogated, since many other talented, and arguably more politically progressive Black male writers have not been similarly singled out.

In this chapter, I argue that the increased critical attention to Charles Johnson's work has, to a large extent, ignored the politics of his fiction, a politics which, I believe, is conservative in terms of both race and gender. Without a critique of the politics of his works, the selection of Johnson for literary canonization cannot be looked at as an entirely promising development in African American literary studies. This chapter examines the directions criticism of Johnson's work has taken and suggests ways that this criticism can be politicized and enriched. My central goal is to find strategies for confronting what I perceive as the reactionary political content of Johnson's work without participating in the general dismissal of African American voices from elite cultural spaces. I begin by considering the philosophical orientation of most of the criticism his work has received.

Three articles on his fiction appearing in *Black American Literature Forum/African American Review*, for example, are so intent on praising Johnson's considerable artistic accomplishments that they eschew any real analysis of the race and gender politics undergirding his fiction. The first of these articles, Ashraf H.A. Rushdy's "The Phenomenology of the Allmuseri: Charles Johnson and the Subject of the Narrative of Slavery," typifies this approach to Johnson's work. Rushdy offers both a fairly accurate representation of some of Johnson's philosophical and political positions, and a good example of the pitfalls encountered by an exclusively praiseful approach to Johnson's work.

Rushdy's analytic strategy is to examine Johnson's "fictions of slavery" using the critical framework laid out in Johnson's non-fiction. The value of such a hermetic hermeneutics is, I think, rather questionable, particularly since Rushdy does not open up Johnson's non-fictional work to critique. Rushdy simply measures the success of Johnson's fiction by the aesthetic/philosophical criteria put forth in Johnson's non-fiction, culminating in his 1988 study, *Being and Race: Black Fiction Since 1970*.[4] The somewhat unfavorable reception of this book puts into question, to an even greater degree, the judiciousness of Rushdy's approach.

While many non-academic reviews praised Johnson's book when it appeared in 1988, its reception in scholarly journals was far less approving.[5] Reviewing the book for *American Literature*, Tom LeClair writes, "Charles Johnson's *Being and Race* is neither written nor edited for a professional academic audience." LeClair's criticism, however, is not strictly "professional"; he additionally notes a gender bias:

> Johnson inclines toward male experimental writers and gives men half again as much space as women even though women writers seem to have dominated the last ten or so years of Afro-American writing. His resentment of the success of Alice Walker's *The Color Purple* is apparent.[6]

The gender problems of *Being and Race* are obscured by the nominally "feminist" statements in Johnson's text, such as his assertions that "the modern emergence of a 'woman's perspective' can only be regarded as a revolutionary, objective step forward in culture and consciousness" (95); or, "women writers of all colors have brought forth a new universal, or way of seeing" (97). But although Johnson is aware that, "like racism, the depths of sexism run deeper than most men dream, sedimenting even our scientific perceptions" (94), his own criticism demonstrates a regrettable gender bias.

For example, Johnson writes in his opening apology to the chapter on Black women writers:

> it would be, I believe, a grave disservice to these writers and to ourselves if we employ a sexual or racial double standard in evaluating their artistic and intellectual successes and failures. I'm speaking of the well-meaning tendency of some critics to use one esthetic or philosophical criterion for evaluating white male authors, usually a tough-minded one, and another, less demanding, for artists nonwhite or female since we are all of us eager to encourage creators who have been forced to overcome an ensemble of racial and cultural obstacles put in the way. But if black women's writing rests on a sound foundation, as I believe some of it does, if it does in fact reveal a common situation

> affecting us all, then the genuine value of the novels and stories we shall address here should be unquestionable, and two sets of criteria, unnecessary. (97)

Johnson's insistence on a single aesthetic standard signals his failure to confront the fullness of feminist critique of literary studies, a large part of which emphasizes the inadequacy of traditional literary evaluative techniques operating under patriarchy to reveal the value of texts by women.

To compound matters, the "tough-minded" criteria Johnson offers as the determinants of the best literature are precisely those which he feels African American women have not met in their writing. The chapter on Black men's writing, for example, opens with this paean to formally innovative art:

> Our most interesting writers are often those who considerably formulate for themselves an esthetic, a project, or ensemble of artistic and cultural problems common to us all...Such a project requires, in some cases, that they transform or personalize the expressive instrument—language—to suit their purposes...this standard of striving is the litmus test we must use to separate the serious artists from the hacks...these artists who are reaching for new ground are often called "experimental"...generally we all benefit from their pioneering, lonely ventures into the realms of the possible, and such artists deserve our gratitude and respect. (57)

Asserting the centrality of experimentation in good writing may not at first seem to carry a gender bias, but once Johnson begins looking at specific writers, the sexism of this criterion becomes clear. Johnson praises "experimental" writers like Clarence Major, Ishmael Reed, Samuel Delany, and David Bradley almost without reservation. When he arrives at his chapter, "The Women," however, his tone changes.

Even the "best" women writers come under attack. Following an opening as promising as "the greatest praise for technical prose mastery among black women must go to the much-celebrated Toni Morrison," Johnson compares her unfavorably to male authors: "I cannot say that she is formally innovative. She has not thematized form in the fashion of Major or Reed. Or offered the kind of intellectual vigor and insight found in Bradley" (101). Criticizing her formal achievements further, Johnson writes:

> one must say of Morrison, as [Arthur P.] Davis does, that "she too often 'tells' us what the characters think and do [and] does not 'render' her material"...artistically, the abstract symbols are not made to live through action, or by the fusing of idea and event...Morrison's fictional universe seems lacking in light and balance. Now again, unsympathetic portraits of whites and also black men surface. These elements are troublesome. (102-3)

Johnson excuses Morrison by saying that "most contemporary fiction by white authors in our time also lacks a masterful sense of dramatic scene" (103).

Morrison's technical shortcomings, especially with regard to "dramatic scene"—a quality which "becomes in the best literary art the very heart of a novel, a story, or a play"—are not, however, hers alone. Despite lavish praise for some aspects of Toni Cade Bambara's writing, Johnson also denies her work the status of "the best literary art," claiming she "falters in her first novel, *The Salt Eaters*, when called upon to achieve "'present-edness' through drama" (103). Likewise, any hint of relenting against Black women writers in Johnson's claim that "it is [Alice Walker's] *The Color Purple*, beyond all doubt, that stands at the crest of black women's fiction in the 1980's" (105) is quickly undermined by his strong criticisms of the novel.[7]

As for the racial politics of *Being and Race*, Norman Harris, in his *Modern Fiction Studies* review, writes:

> Although he wrestles with important questions that all people must face, Johnson seems to feel it necessary to strip himself of his own culture so that he may then see. Maybe he should heed the advice of the heroine in his novel, *Faith and the Good Thing*, and "hook-up" with the Wherewitch so that the circle of cultural continuity and development will not be broken.[8]

I will pursue the racial implications of Johnson's aesthetics at greater length below. For the moment, it must suffice to say that, while one should not accept these critiques of *Being and Race* as decisive simply because they appear in scholarly journals, the serious race and gender concerns these reviews raise should give the user of *Being and Race* pause.

Unfortunately, Rushdy glosses over these concerns. The critical starting point for his article is instead Johnson's conception of the writing/reading process. Rushdy writes:

> Johnson offers us a poetics in which the art of reading becomes the act of inhabiting the role and place of others, and the art of writing requires an authorial "act of self-surrender" of such magnitude that the writer finds her or his "perceptions and experiences" coinciding with ones that preceded her or him.[9]

Johnson argues, however, that textually under/misrepresented writers within this literary system face the disheartening choice either to "inhabit" available (almost exclusively White male) roles which are incompatible with their own lived ones or to stake out crudely defined oppositional positions. The writer who does not wish to occupy either position finds himself in a dilemma—"Caliban's dilemma." Rushdy identifies this concept with Calibanic models from the works of James Baldwin and Houston A. Baker, Jr.[10]

Johnson argues that African American fiction writers almost always accede to this dualism rather than refuse or transcend it. As a result, Johnson suggests, they are caught up in a restrictive mode of reactive racialized thinking, and the quality of their work has suffered. Johnson ends his sketch of the history of African American fiction in the first chapter of *Being and Race* with a rather negative assessment, drawing on the conservative criticism of Ralph Ellison:

> Throughout the control-of-images argument [which Johnson associates with the writers of the Harlem Renaissance], Negritude, and Cultural Nationalism, this "pre-individualistic" tendency emerges again and again. "The pre-individualistic black," writes Ellison, "discourages individuality out of self-defense. Having learned through experience that the whole group is punished for the actions of the single member, it has worked out efficient techniques for behavior control." Obviously, it cannot be through such ideologies that genuine creative work is achieved. Rather, all presuppositions, all theories, must be suspended before experience and meaning can be brought forth in black literary art. (29)

Johnson's belief that "genuine creative work" can only emerge from the privatized sphere of the bourgeois individual writes out of the canon of great art the mass of African American literature, most of which has emerged from a sense of collective identity and shared racial experience. Rushdy, unfortunately, endorses this implicit condemnation of much, if not most, twentieth century African American literature and moves on to explicate Johnson's program for transcending the Calibanic problem.

Rushdy writes, "The answer to Caliban's dilemma in Johnson's career as a writer of fiction, has been to write a theory of intersubjectivity into his 'four narratives of slavery'" (375). Rushdy names Johnson's theory of intersubjectivity "the phenomenology of the Allmuseri" after the fictional African tribe appearing in several of Johnson's works. Allmuseri intersubjectivity is achieved through what Johnson calls the "transcendence of relativism," a process which Rushdy explains in the following way:

> Not only does it articulate a form of transcendence in which intersubjective relations are made possible, in which "relativism" is a condition of being open to the other and others' ideas; but it also suggests that this transcendence is part of an overall project in which "relativism" will be transcended, in which "intersubjective experience" will supersede what, since Kant, has been criticized as being merely "subjective experience." (376)

Johnson's philosophical schema accepts the existence of difference, including racial difference, only as a moment in the movement towards a higher Hegelian unity. The Allmuseri, as the cultural embodiment of this philosophy, exemplify its teleological goal of final eradication of difference. Rushdy writes:

> According to Allmuseri phenomenology, the individual subject's ideal condition involves the renunciation of being situated in the material world. In other words, the ideal of intersubjectivity includes the condition of the individual's being "unpositioned" in the world, of each person's having relationship with the tribal community that is so integral that the individual is rendered "invisible" in the "presence of others." Like "writing," as Johnson theorizes, this is a form of intersubjectivity—the sharing of the "same cultural Lifeworld," a "common situation, a common history"—which is premised on the "transcendence of relativism." (377)

The Allmuseri are not the only means Johnson has used to explore his philosophy; he has elaborated his ideas in a number of cultural contexts. In an article I examine below, William Gleason describes how Zen Buddhism offers Johnson another model for achieving a state of undifferentiation. In his critical writings, Johnson uses Husserlian phenomenology in yet another formulation to explain his philosophical/aesthetic position. In the 1980 article, "Philosophy and Black Fiction," he writes:

> A *fresh* encounter with Black life requires: (1) All presuppositions, whatever we think we know about Black life, all our cherished beliefs in what is and how it appears must be suspended, shelved, "bracketed." Aspects of the Black world become, after the *epoche*, only the occasion for universal reflection. (2) With this "bracketing" accomplished, Black experience becomes a pure field of appearances with but two important poles: consciousness and the objects, others, to which it is related intentionally. We describe *how* these appear, and note that Black subjectivity (memory, desire, anticipation, will) stain [!] them with a particular sense...(3) Finally, we ask if this look at Black life—stripped in the first stage of all Black particulars, purified or irrealized such that it now stands before us as an instance of *all* experience...of its type...Surely, it must.[11]

In this schema, the Hegelian character of the "transcendence of relativism" becomes most clear. Black subjects first eradicate their individuality through submersion in Black communal life, then transcend that life by moving into a universal experience of raceless Being. This idealistic phenomenology enables Johnson to simultaneously champion the contradictory ideals of racial communitarianism and transcendent racelessness.

I argue, in contrast to Rushdy's philosophical, appreciative approach, however, that Johnson's phenomenological conception of literary experience opens up considerable political problems in his work. First of all, lines of philosophical thought too numerous to discuss have discredited notions of phenomenological "bracketing" as impossibly idealistic.[12] As for the possibilities of Buddhist or Allmuseri transcendence, such speculation is beyond the purview of my literary criticism. What this chapter will argue, however, is that Johnson's own fictional worlds belie any possibility of a universal phenomenological reduction. Even without a rigorous philosophical debunking of the notion of "transcendence of relativism," it is apparent, when one looks at Johnson's fiction, that his conception of intersubjectivity fails in its bid for universality since, as I will demonstrate, it embraces no identity positions other than those of Johnson's central male characters. The abandonment of self which Johnson claims accompanies the intersubjective joining with others, turns out—and this is my central argument—to consist in little more than Johnson's male protagonists—usually Black, but in some cases, White—identifying with the dominant ideology of their milieus: always, White supremacist patriarchy.

William Gleason's *African American Review* article on *Oxherding Tale* parallels Rushdy's in its accession to Johnson's personal critical objectives. After noting that Johnson has called for Black fiction "achieving 'whole sight,' a broadened literary outlook that embraces (to quote Clayton Riley) 'the entire world—not just the fractured world of American racism and psychic social disorder,'" Gleason states that his own goal is to argue "that Johnson's second novel, *Oxherding Tale*, is an explicit response to his own call."[13] By straightjacketing himself within the critical parameters determined in advance by Johnson, Gleason effectively dismisses any critical or political positions which are not Johnson's own. As a result, in his analysis of a novel full of negative representations of women, Gleason's only mention of gender politics comes in a final, single sentence footnote ("One should note, however, that, in the novel itself, despite all the moves away from essence, *woman* seems to get re-essentialized as being.").

Gleason's more extended discussion of race amounts to little more than an effort to silence serious inquiry into the race politics of Johnson's fiction. He writes, for instance:

> If, however, we maintain that an affirmative reading of *Oxherding Tale's* ending [in which the central black character passes as a white man] means that Johnson is trapped by structures he seeks to undermine, we will still want to ask whether he is aware of the trap. Frankly, I think he is; but I also think he would claim that his particular vision of a new Afro-American literature not only requires such an ending, but also transcends the trap. It requires such an ending in *this* novel because, for Johnson, literature concerns itself with "*this* person in *this* situation." Johnson calls for fictions that "believe in the interchangeability of standpoints; we throw ourselves *with* a character toward his projects, divest ourselves of our own historically acquired peculiarities, and reconstruct his world." Given what we learn of Andrew, it is at least plausible that he would pass—and enjoy it. (We may object that no one can completely divest himself of, well, his self, but someone who has had a Zen experience of enlightenment might—as might someone—like Johnson, and like Andrew—who wants to deconstruct essences, including race and gender). (724)

Gleason raises the highly charged issue of racial "passing" only to sweep it under the political carpet through recourse to Johnson's "particular vision of a new Afro-American literature" and a hypothetical "Zen experience of enlightenment." By blinding himself to any critical perspective other than Johnson's, Gleason effectively silences readings which would interrogate the implication of an "affirmative" representation of Andrew's passing.[14]

In a third article, also on *Oxherding Tale*, Jennifer Hayward, while falling prey to a similar tendency to celebrate Johnson rather than critique him, nevertheless raises urgent concerns about the gender politics of Johnson's fiction. In her 1991 piece, "Something to Serve: Constructs of the Feminine in Charles Johnson's *Oxherding Tale*," Hayward opens by asserting the existence of a feminist consciousness in this novel stating that "*Oxherding Tale* acknowledges the marginalization not only of black men but of women, black and white."[15] At the same time, however, Hayward reveals the sexist content of *Oxherding Tale*. Near the end of the article's introduction she notes:

> Johnson's attitude towards women tends towards a glorification of the Eternal Feminine, an attitude which can (and, in this book, several times does) flip over into the concomitant terror of women as all-encompassing and all-powerful. (690)

But firm in her belief in Johnson's good faith feminism, Hayward follows this expression of concern with praise:

> The fact nevertheless remains that Johnson makes a strong attempt to understand feminist issues and to inscribe them in his book. And his technical innovations—particularly the shifts in narrative and temporal perspective—help break the bounds of canonical (Western androcentric) literature. (690)

Hayward's backstepping "the fact nevertheless remains" comes to feel artificial, even patronizing, as one proceeds through her devastating reading of the sexual politics of *Oxherding Tale*. She compiles a fairly thorough catalogue of the novel's gender problems: the reduction of women to violent, insentient Nature, voyeuristic depictions of their physical destruction, and the placement of "positive" female characters in conventionally feminine roles. Nevertheless, she ultimately gives Johnson a feminist "thumbs up" for his efforts. In the final lines of her essay, she writes that the novel's "irreducible complexity and self-contradiction (and even, in a sense, its collapsed vision of women) can be read as strengths, adding to the evocative power of this strange and fascinating book" (703). At this point, even the sexism of a "collapsed vision of women" in *Oxherding Tale* becomes a "strength."

For my own purposes, I will focus on the body of Hayward's essay, where she is more critical of Johnson's gender politics than her framing remarks suggest. In Johnson's play with slave narrative conventions, for example, Hayward points out a gender reversal in *Oxherding Tale's* representation of the slave family. She writes:

> Andrew's genealogy recalls, and inverts, the conventional paradigm of a protagonist of mixed blood, split between house and field, with an absent or repudiating (white) father and an all-powerful and supportive (black) mother or grandmother. Andrew's birth mother, plantation owner Anna Polkinghorne, refuses to acknowledge him; his adoptive mother, slave Mattie Hawkins, seems almost equally distant; on the other hand, both his master Jonathan Polkinghorne and his father George Hawkins claim and nurture him. (690)

Later in her article, Hayward interrogates the possible sexism of such inversions of the slave narrative tradition:

> Johnson significantly reverses the classic slave narrative by giving Andrew two strongly supportive fathers and no mother. This is just one indication (and, perhaps, partial explanation) of Andrew's (and Johnson's) conflicted attitude towards women. (697)

Hayward rightly questions the implications of a reversal whose structure suggests that the slave Andrew's real antagonist is not his White owner, but hostile "mothers," White and Black.

Johnson enacts a similar reversal in his representation of the more serious issue of the rape of slaves. Despite the fact that it is a result of a secret wife-swapping arrangement between Andrew's father George and his Master, Johnson renders the sexual encounter between George and his Mistress Anna Polkinghorne in a way so as to suggest George's unwillingness and Anna's aggression. Johnson writes:

> What happened next, he had not expected. Sleepily, Anna turned and soldered herself to George. She crushed him in a clinch so strong his spine cracked. Now he had fallen too far to stop. She talked to George, a wild stream of gibberish, which scared him plenty, but he was not a man to leave his chores half-finished, and plowed on.[16]

Anna becomes a pseudo-rapist, "soldering herself to George," who is "scared," overpowering him with "a clinch so strong his spine cracked." While this comic scene hints that George enjoys the sexual act, Anna is nevertheless cast as the powerful aggressor.[17] In this way, White women are directly implicated in the sexual violation of slaves. This blame is even more pronounced in the presentation of Flo Hatfield.

In another bit of "play" with the history of slave rape, Johnson creates Flo Hatfield, the "black widow" figure in *Oxherding Tale*, as a stand-in for the violent male Master/rapist of traditional slave narratives. We are introduced to her sexually predatory and murderous habits in Andrew's father's first description of her:

> Traveling with me to Abbeville, George told a story, very strange, of Flo Hatfield's appetites. A widow, forty if a day, she lived on a five-

hundred-acre farm—she called it Leviathan—and often picked a slave, preferably male, from her fields...For days, whole weeks, Flo Hatfield entertained him—how George couldn't figure, but eventually a black Maria eased in from town, and a veterinarian examined the body. Then a mortician dragged a pine casket down her front steps, hauled it away, and her bondsman was listed among slaves who'd fled to Canada. (20)

In her search for sexual satisfaction, Flo Hatfield drives Patrick, Andrew's predecessor, to suicide. Patrick's own predecessor, a runaway named Moon, is returned dead by a slavecatcher, his death linked to Flo's sexual exploitation of him. Noting "the green stains on [Moon's] groin, gas ballooning his genitalia in a ghastly parody of eros" (67), Andrew speculates on the connection between Moon's death and Flo's sexual use of him:

> Was this horror the coda of pleasure? There was, it seemed to me, something especially hideous in this end to enlightened hedonism, for the johnson (as we say—pronounced *yawn-sun*) of the lover expanded to Rabelaisian proportions, the testicles bloated bigger than coconuts, as if Death mocked a man's single distinguishing feature by enlarging the genitals, exploded and powdered them green with breadmold: a nest for maggots. (69)

Given that traditional slave narratives present a race and gender landscape reported by actual slaves, Johnson's play with the gender tropes of these narratives cannot be accepted as mere formal innovations. His gender reversals do offer a number of provocative suggestions for understanding the complex relationships between slaves and their owners: a challenge to the "innocence" of slaveholding women; a reminder of the sometimes forgotten sexual violation of male slaves[18]; an assertion of agency or desire on the part of White women (albeit, quite problematic) in the face of ideology which defined them as passive. These interpretations do not, however, interrupt a reading of Johnson's inversions which suggest the physical, especially sexual, victimization of men by women. And we must critique such representations of gender insofar as they obscure the historical sexual exploitation of women, especially Black women, by men and deny the role that Black women have played in maintaining community under oppressive conditions like slavery.

What makes the political function of the character of Flo Hatfield difficult to grasp is the fact that while she is clearly the most violent and oppressive slaveowner in the novel, she also lays claim to an oppression analogous to that of slaves. In one of her speeches to Andrew, she says:

> People say a woman is *nothing* without a man! A kind of freak to be pitied! A failure—people tell you—in the grand scheme of things! The bastards. Maybe you *do* know...Years ago I thought colored men were closer to seeing through this than anybody. Now...I'm not so sure. You've suffered, but you've never been married to someone so stupid he felt threatened if you sat on top, had an opinion, or knew how to

tell time. In six years of marriage I didn't come *once...Even* acting helpless doesn't make a difference. You still get old. You get fat. Or too thin. You have female trouble. Your hair falls out and your husband starts fucking everything under the age of twenty-five...*I used* to be beautiful.... (59)

The novel's Allmuseri character, Reb the Coffinmaker, agrees with Flo's self-assessment, saying to Andrew, "She's a slave like you'n me...Without you, she don't know who she *is*...you ain't nothin' without somethin'—or somebody—to serve" (62). Hayward uses Reb's statement in the title of her essay and as the central trope for understanding the racial/gender politics of *Oxherding Tale*. The novel, she argues, can be understood as the process of Andrew's discovery that life's meaning lies in finding "something to serve." While she quotes Reb to support her argument, however, she questions the accuracy of the Coffinmaker's easy analogy between Flo and Andrew.

Hayward observes that even as Johnson draws a comparison between women under patriarchy and race slaves, he writes a text in which "Andrew's women repeatedly break the bounds of this politically correct racial/feminist parallel" (698). Even as *Oxherding Tale* identifies women with racially subordinated slaves, it links them to Nature, before which men, enslaved or free, are helpless. In this way, women, White and Black, assume a position of dominance over Black men. Hayward writes that "Andrew's fear of women seems to be tied to his attitude towards slavery: both threaten a loss of Self. Love of a woman is in fact explicitly paralleled to slavery" (701). Hayward thus subverts the parallel between White women and slaves she has proposed with the conflicting claim that in Johnson's text African American men are subordinated to both Whites and women.

Hayward's insights seem, in the end, to lead further than her article is willing to go. In the world of *Oxherding Tale*, slavery *per se* turns out to be less antagonistic to Black men than are women. The White men in the novel generally play a beneficent role in the Black male characters' lives. Andrew's father, for example, has a strong friendship with his owner which is broken only by their spouses' resentment over the wife-swapping trick with which the novel opens. Master Polkinghorne nevertheless pampers Andrew. Even putatively threatening White men end up having a profound, even educational role in Andrew's life. The most extravagant villain in the novel (with the possible exception of Flo Hatfield), for example, the murderous slave catcher, the Soulcatcher, far from killing Andrew or returning him to slavery, ultimately has an educational role in his development. The novel ends with Andrew swimming in the shifting mosaic of the Soulcatcher's tattooed body, discovering the interconnectedness of all things in universal Being.

The women in *Oxherding Tale*, on the other hand, offer little but antagonism to Andrew. Those who do not mistreat him outright disappear in a vacuum of death or anonymity. Minty, Andrew's slave lover, conveniently dies once Andrew finds happiness passing for White with a White wife. This wife, Peggy, whom Johnson first represents in a nominally non-sexist manner (she is bookish and attractive to Andrew without being "pretty"), soon finds herself happily relegated to the role of submissive, though comically incompetent, servant to her husband. By the final pages of the novel, Andrew has ceased referring to her by anything other than the third person designation, "Wife."

In the end, Johnson establishes the identity of Black men not around an antagonism to Whiteness and femininity, but only to femininity. Johnson posits a transcendentally unbridgeable division between men and women which tends to resolve itself through the subordination of men. Hayward sees this dynamic at work in *Oxherding Tale*:

> By the end of the book, Andrew does seem to have overcome the dichotomy of black versus white, but only by figuring both black and white *men*, as opposed to women. He feels "an ancient war" or "crisis in the male spirit" unfolding equally in his father's cabin and in his master's house, with the women, somehow, perceived as coming out on top. (699-700)

Following Hayward, I argue that Andrew's ostensible search for "something to serve," by linking women to Whites via their power over Black men, obscures another ideological alignment going on in *Oxherding Tale* and much of the rest of Johnson's fiction: the pitting of men against women through the denial of the racial inequities which might problematize a simplistic division of the sexes.[19]

Throughout his fiction, Johnson articulates women as the antagonists of men—often at those sites most strongly associated with the subjugation of women. In his 1986 collection of short stories, *The Sorcerer's Apprentice and Other Stories*, for example, one finds an account of sexual harassment in the story, "Aletheia." Johnson tells the story of a male professor's harassment by a female student. While the tale suggests that the professor learns and grows from the experience, by representing the female student as the harasser, Johnson's story opens itself to appropriation by anti-feminist efforts to obscure the much more serious problem of male sexual harassment of women. The student in "Aletheia" tells the hapless professor:

> I'd do *any*thing to get that grade...I know how this place works...I ain't *about* to go back to no factory, or day-work. If I don't ace this course—are you listenin'?—I'm gonna have to tell your chairman Dick Dunn and Dean David McCracken that you been houndin' me for trim...if I flunk...you're finished...I *can* be nice, too, you know, once you get to know me.[20]

The professor responds:

> She was armed with endless tricks and strategies, this black girl, but Wendy was nobody's fool—she used Niggerese playfully, like a toy, to bait, to draw me out. She was a witch, yes. A thug. But she had me, rightly or wrongly, at bay. (106)

Near the end of the story he characterizes the student as "the girl who shotgunned me with blackmail back at Padelford Hall, who made me jump like a trained seal" (111). "Aletheia," it must be stressed, makes no claim to represent the larger issue of harassment, but the regularity, throughout both this collection and Johnson's body of fiction, of such inverted representations of sexual power articulates a vision of gender relations which makes feminist arguments for gender equity seem irrational.

In "Menagerie, A Child's Fable," Johnson reverses the power dynamic of an even more serious site of sexist practice. Here, Johnson not only trivializes and parodies rape and a feminist response to it, but turns the rape victim and her female supporters into the violent antagonists of men. In the story, a male Siamese cat rapes a female rabbit. Johnson writes:

> Rabbit took this badly. In the beginning she sniffed a great deal, and with good reason—rape was a vicious thing—but her grief and pain got out of hand, and soon she was lost in it with no way out, like a child in a dark forest, and began organizing the females of every species to stop cohabiting with the males. [The watchdog] stood back, afraid to butt in because Rabbit said that it was none of his damned business and he was as bad as all the rest. (54)

The narrator's offhand remark, "rape was a vicious thing," loses whatever force it might have as he ridicules the rabbit's "feminist" response as "out of hand." First, Rabbit considers aborting the pregnancy resulting from this rape (the imminent product of which the narrator glibly refers to as "the cabbit"). By the end, the female animals have "torn Siamese to pieces" (58). In the absence of any less flippant representation of rape or parodic rendering of feminism, Johnson's artistic choice here again opens itself up to political alignment with the worst sexist and anti-feminist discourses.

"Menagerie" also exemplifies the way Johnson's gender politics link up with conservative positions on race. Johnson places this anti-feminist rape scenario in the context of a broad argument against multiculturalism. "Menagerie, A Children's Fable" is meant, as its title suggests, to teach some kind of lesson, in this case, one regarding the dangers of integrating previously separated groups or individuals. The story tells of the destruction of a pet store whose owner one day disappears. The protagonist of the story, a German Shepherd watchdog named Berkeley, reluctantly lets the animals out of their cages:

> The animals clamored for release; they took up Monkey's cry, "Self-determination!" But everything within Berkeley resisted this idea, the possibility of chaos it promised, so many different, quarrelsome creatures uncaged...The chances for mischief were incalculable, no question of that, but slow starvation was certain if he didn't let them in the storeroom. Furthermore, he didn't want to be called a fascist. It didn't seem fair, Monkey saying that, making him look bad in front of others. It was the one charge you couldn't defend yourself against. (48)

By naming the cage-opening dog "Berkeley," Johnson locates the story's allegorical target even more specifically as campus multiculturalism.

"Menagerie"'s implicit position against multiculturalism in places of learning becomes clear in the final horrific "Balkanization" of the pet shop. After the disappearance of its cruel but stabilizing patriarch, Mr. Tilford, the animals' efforts towards "self-determination" lead to their destruction by fire. Johnson writes:

> The corrosion grew day by day. Cracks, then fissures began to appear, it seemed to Berkeley, everywhere, and in places where he least expected them. Puddles and pyramidal plops were scattered underfoot like traps. Bacterial flies were everywhere. Then came maggots. Hamsters gnawed at electrical cords in the storeroom. Frog fell sick with a genital infection. The fish, though the gentlest of creatures, caused undertow by demanding day-and-night protection, claiming they were handicapped in the competition for food, confined to their tanks, and besides, they were from the most ancient tree; all life came from the sea, they argued, the others owed *them*.
> Old blood feuds between beasts erupted, too, grudges so tired you'd have thought them long buried, but not so. (53-4)

This passage glosses many of the tropes conservatives typically exploit to discredit multiculturalism. Besides general disorder there are suggestions of the ungratefulness towards Western advances (the hamsters' destruction of electrical cords), moral/sexual collapse (the frog's "genital infection") and unreasonable group-based demands for preferential treatment and claims of historico-cultural superiority (all found in the fishes' Afrocentric-sounding charges and their request for Civil Rights-type protection).

The story's parallel parodies of feminist and multicultural concerns serve, through a logic of contiguity, to enhance the mutual discrediting of feminism and multiculturalism. "Menagerie" furthermore places such positions in a relationship of equivalence which articulates, through a process of negation, an unparodied masculinist "race-blind" position. In these ways, the story condenses a discourse which simultaneously denies the relevance of race and pits men against women. Similarly discrediting conflations of feminist and anti-racist politics can be found in other stories in *The Sorcerer's Apprentice*.

The simultaneous articulation of women as antagonists to men and a call for the transcendence of the "fiction of race" structures the seemingly apolitical narrative of personal growth in the story "China." "China" opens with the portrait of a sickly middle aged black couple. Johnson links the husband's declining health to the disappointments he has encountered in life:

> [Rudolph] kept his dissatisfaction to himself, but occasionally Evelyn would glimpse in his eyes that look, that distant, pained expression that asked: Is this all? She saw it after her first miscarriage, then her second; saw it when he stopped searching the want ads and settled on the Post Office as the fulfillment of his potential in the marketplace. It was always there, that look, after he turned forty, and no new, lavishly praised novel from the Book-of-the-Month Club, no feature-length movie, prayer meeting, or meal she fixed for him wiped it from Rudolph's eyes. (78-9)

Rudolph's disappointments, surprisingly, are never connected to his race. In fact, the failures he does enumerate all emphasize the innocence of White people. When Boeing is said to be "hiring Black men," Rudolph fails to get the job because of his health, the poorness of which, as I argue below, Johnson blames on implicit cultural pathologies of the African American community in which he has lived. Rudolph's only other professional rejection specifically mentioned in the story comes from a Black Bible college.

Rudolph's life begins to change, however, after he sees a martial arts movie. Excited by what he has witnessed, he joins a *kwoon* to study *gung-fu*. The resulting improvements in his body are miraculous:

> apparently he was doing something right. Dr. Guylee's examination had been glowing; he said Rudolph's muscle tone, whatever that was, was better. His cardiovascular system was healthier...Evelyn, even she, saw in the crepuscular light changes in Rudolph's upper body as he stretched: Muscles like globes of light rippled along his shoulders; larval currents moved on his belly. The language of his new developing body eluded her...This new flesh had the contours of the silhouetted figures on medical charts: the body as it must be in the mind of God. (83-4)

Not only does he regain his bodily health, Rudolph achieves a spiritual peace which had until this point eluded him. He tells his wife:

> *Gung-fu* means "hard work" in Chinese...I don't think I've ever really done hard work in my life. Not like this, something that asks me to give everything, body and soul, spirit and flesh...I've never been able to give everything to anything. The world never let me. Do you know what I'm saying? Every job I've ever had, everything I've ever done, it only demanded part of me. It was like there was so much *more* of me that went unused after the job was over. I get that feeling in church

sometimes...Sometimes I get that feeling with you...There's a part of me left over. You never tried to touch all of me, to take everything. Maybe you can't. Maybe no one can. But sometimes I get the feeling that the unused part—the unlived life—*spoils*, that you get cancer because it sits like fruit on the ground and rots...Don't ask me to stop training...If I stop, I'll die. (76)

Through his physical and mental exercises, Rudolph creates for himself a metaphysical experience roughly analogous to the "transcendence of relativism" discussed above. Johnson writes:

> He'd never breathed before, he told her. Not once. Not clear to the floor of himself. Never breathed and emptied himself as he did now, picturing himself sitting on the bottom of Lake Washington: himself, Rudolph Lee Jackson, at the center of the universe; for if the universe was infinite, any point where he stood would be at its center—it would shift and move with him...He told her that in *zazen*, at the bottom of the lake, he worked to discipline his mind and maintain one point of concentration; each thought, each feeling that overcame him he saw as a fragile bubble, which he could inspect passionlessly from all sides; then he let it float gently to the surface, and soon—as he slipped deeper into the vortices of himself, into the Void—even the image he had of himself on the lake floor vanished. (87)

Able to transcend the particularities of mundane existence, he gains a superhuman sense of peace:

> Rudolph, she saw, didn't want anything; everything, Evelyn included, delighted him, but as far as Rudolph was concerned, it was all shadows in a phantom history. He was humbler now, more patient, but he'd lost touch with everything she knew was normal in people: weakness, fear, guilt, self-doubt, the very things that gave the world thickness and made people do things. (89)

"China" thus acts as a sort of before-and-after advertisement for Johnson's program for self-renunciation. Another reading of this story, however, supports my claim that the kind of transcendence Johnson advocates in Allmuseri phenomenology, Zen Buddhism, Husserlian phenomenology or, here, *gung fu*, offers little to women and poses no challenge to White supremacist hegemony. Rudolph's struggle turns out to be not simply with the materialist values with which he has been raised, but is explicitly with the gendered, raced embodiment of those values: his wife, Evelyn. As in other stories in *The Sorcerer's Apprentice*, the central male figure's antagonist is a woman. Rudolph's initial ill-health, while implicitly blamed on the bad hand life has dealt him, ultimately is connected to Evelyn's treatment of him.

Part of his improved condition, for example, derives from the adoption of a healthier diet than the one Evelyn has been offering him. The story opens with Rudolph suffering from shortness of breath, a result, the narrator says, of "an allergy to something she put in his food perhaps" (63). After his "conversion," Rudolph "cooked his own meals, called her heavy soul dishes 'too acidic,' lived on raw vegetables, seaweed, nuts, and fruit to make his body 'more alkaline,' and fasted on Sundays" (79). As for his increased exercise, although it seems to have saved his life, Evelyn opposes it; instead, "she preferred him falling asleep in his chair beside her, as he used to" (86). At one point, she accidentally reveals to her husband how she really feels about his improved condition: "Rudolph, I want you back the way you were: *sick*" (89). The story even goes so far as to suggest that Evelyn wants not just a sick Rudolph, but to be free of him altogether. The night he disappears to see the martial arts film, the narrator reports that for Evelyn, "it felt good not to have him underfoot, a little like he was dead already. But the last thing Evelyn wanted was that or, as she lay down against her lumpy backrest, to fall asleep, though she did..." (71). The ambiguous relation of the final clause, "though she did," to her two previous thoughts—not wanting to sleep and not wanting to be free of Rudolph—creepily inflects her attitude toward her husband.

"China"'s stark differentiation between his wife's ill effect on Rudolph and the miraculously positive influence of the all-male kwoon takes on an explicitly racial character as well. Much of the danger that Evelyn putatively poses to Rudolph grows out of her participation in the African American community described in the story. Johnson juxtaposes Rudolph's physical improvements to Evelyn's participation in parodic examples of Black culture, noting, for example, that as Rudolph "walked around the house in his Everlast leg weights, tried push-ups on his fingers and wrists...she sat trying to watch 'The Jeffersons'" (85-6). Again, Rudolph's avoidance of Evelyn's "heavy soul food" improves his health. Even the Black church, an early influence in Rudolph's life, is represented, finally, as a disappointment. It is, in fact, the church's rejection of him that may have begun his physical and emotional decline. Johnson writes: "Rudolph had begun to run down, Evelyn decided, the minute he was turned down by Moody Bible Institute" (69).

What charges of racism there are in the story are turned on Evelyn. Attempting to identify Asian actors, the narrator, in a free indirect discursive style meant to capture the nuance of Evelyn's attitude, reports that "she couldn't tell those people apart" (65). Her allegiance to a pessimistic, self-destructive lifestyle is embodied by the White religious symbol on her wall: "a bearded white carpenter impaled on a rood...in this timeless image she felt comforted that suffering was inescapable, the loss of vitality inevitable, even a good thing maybe" (70).

By contrast, Rudolph is presented as "color-blind." The new friends he makes in his *gung fu* kwoon are a veritable rainbow: Vietnamese, Chinese, Puerto Rican, White (but, notably, other than Rudolph, no Black members are mentioned). In "China"'s martial arts community, race and class prejudices fall by the wayside. His new friends embrace Rudolph in a way that the race-conscious Evelyn cannot understand:

> they liked him. They were separated by money, background, and religion, but something she could not identify made them seem, those nights on the porch after his class, like a single body. (82)

When Evelyn tries to remind Rudolph of his background, her reminder is presented as an attempt to racially restrict Rudolph's expanding sense of Being:

> "You grew up in Hodges, South Carolina, same as me, in a right and proper colored church. If you'd been to China, maybe I'd understand."
> "I can only be what I've been?" This he asked softly, but his voice trembled. "Only what I was in Hodges?"
> "You can't be Chinese."
> "I don't want to be Chinese!...I only want to be what I can be, which isn't the greatest fighter in the world, only the fighter I can be." (90-1)

The story rightly interrogates Evelyn's either/or logic of cultural identification; it does not, however, examine Rudolph's assertion that being "what he *can* be" entails the virtual repudiation of his native African American culture. In the end, Rudolph's wholehearted embrace of Asian martial arts culture is presented as nothing short of salvational. On the final page, Evelyn, who had earlier "known in her bones" that "he would die before her," now realizes that "he would outlive her."

It is in the collection's first story, "The Education of Mingo," however, that Johnson creates his scariest scenario of race-blind male bonding—here, literally, over a dead female body. In this story, an "amiable" slave-owner, Moses Green, buys a male slave and raises him as if he were a son. Green instructs Mingo so well, in fact, that he becomes something of Moses' *doppelganger*. One of "The Education of Mingo"'s central arguments is that an identity doubling effect occurs when one person owns another. This idea is a provocative one and Johnson explores it in a fascinating manner. Moses' relationship with Mingo, however, cannot fully be grasped as one simply of ownership; it must be considered both in its racial character and as it is defined against Moses' relationship with a woman, Harriet Bridgewater.

Moses is drawn to "his lady friend," Harriet, in spite of her lack of conventional beauty:

> She wasn't exactly pretty, what with her gull's nose, great heaps of red-gold hair, and frizzy down on her arms, but she had a certain silvery beauty intangible, elusive, inside...She knew things, that shrewd Harriet Bridgewater. (8)

For all this elusive attraction, however, Moses' considerably stronger bond with his male slave quickly becomes apparent:

> strange to say, [Moses] felt closer to the black African than to Harriet. So close, in fact, that when he pulled the rig up to Isaiah's house, he considered giving Mingo his farm when he died, God willing, as well as his knowledge, beliefs, and prejudices. Then again, maybe that was overdoing things. The boy was all Moses wanted him to be, his own emanation, but still, he thought, himself. Different enough from Moses so that he could step back and admire him. (11)

Moses' preference for Mingo cannot be understood as simple narcissism, for while Moses enjoys the resemblance which grows up between him and Mingo, Moses resists a similar relationship of intimacy with Harriet, from fear that he will grow to resemble her:

> Y'know, I was gonna ask you to marry me this morning...but I figured living alone was better when I thoughta how married folks—and sometimes wimmin with dogs—got to favoring each other...like they was wax candles flowing together. (20)

Fears of intermingling do not prevent him from accepting a lifelong intimacy with the slave Mingo, however. Moses muses:

> how in blazes could he disengage himself when Mingo shored up, sustained, let be Moses's world with all its sores and blemishes every time he opened his oily black eyes? Thanks to the trouble he took cementing Mingo to his own mind, he could not, by thunder, do without him now. Giving him his freedom, handing it to him like a rasher of bacon, would shackle Mingo to him even more. (19-20)

Once again the gulf between men and women is presented as impossible, or at least distasteful, to bridge, while the connection between men, even across a barrier as seemingly insurmountable as enslavement, emerges as inevitable and desirable.

This point is violently confirmed by the end of the story. Along with the better parts of his personality, Moses instills in Mingo his own evil desires. In the process, he creates an evil double who will commit despicable acts about which Moses fantasizes, but which he cannot perform. He explains this to Mingo:

> Mingo, you more me than I am myself. Me planed away to the bone! Ya understand?...All the wrong, all the good you do, now or tomorrow—it's me indirectly doing it, but without the lies and excuses, without the feeling what's its foundation, with all the polite make-up and apologies removed. It's an empty gesture, like the swing of a shadow's arm. You can't never see things exactly the way I do. I'm guilty. It was me set the gears in motion. Me.... (22)

Understanding their relationship in a similar way, Mingo explains that in raping and murdering Harriet Bridgewater he was only carrying out Moses' wishes:

> "Talky old hen daid now, boss."
> The old man's face shattered. "I was gonna marry that woman!"
> "Naw." Mingo frowned. From out of his frown a huge grin flowered.
> "You say—I'm quoting you now, suh—a man needs a quiet, patient, uncomplaining woman, right?" (21)

Moses is upset by Mingo's crime and considers shooting him. The story's final tableau, however, makes the ultimate nature of Moses' affection clear: he and Mingo ride away from Harriet's raped and murdered body for a fugitive life together in Missouri.

In his most recent work, the novel *Middle Passage*, Johnson explores the possibilities of interracial male homosociality fully. *Middle Passage's* Black protagonist, Rutherford Calhoun, spends the majority of the novel on board a slave ship with its attendant all-male crew. This gender segregated arrangement allows Johnson to naturalize an eternal division between men and women. Indeed, the novel opens with these lines: "Of all the things that drive men to sea, the most common disaster, I've come to learn, is women."[21] As harrowing as the prospect of a Black man's stowing away on a slave ship should (and turns out to) be, Rutherford fears the "disaster" of Isadora Bailey more. Rather than submit to the marriage into which she attempts to blackmail him, he embarks on an adventure so horrifying that it teaches Rutherford to resign all claims to Selfhood in programmatic Johnson fashion.

As pregnant with possibilities for examining race as is a Black man's adventures on a slave ship, Johnson undercuts the significance of race rather than explore how it functions. Johnson plays down the most evident racial difference on the ship—that between the slaves and the crew—by writing that the enslaved Africans "were not even 'Negroes.' They were Allmuseri" (76). The central plot acts even more aggressively to deny the significance of race. Johnson structures Rutherford's adventure ultimately to reveal to him the lie of all attempts at racial differentiation. The means for revealing this to him are, as in other Johnson pieces, a series of cross-racial male pairings.

Like Andrew and Mingo, Rutherford is blessed with an incredibly supportive White "father." Rutherford describes him thus:

> he was, in most senses of the word, a fair, sympathetic, and well-meaning man, as whites go. In all North America, if you searched up and down, you'd not likely find a more reluctant slave owner than he—one who inherited us and hated the Peculiar Institution—and we knew fortune could have treated us far worse. (111)

To compensate for their enslavement, Master Chandler educates Rutherford and his brother in a fashion similar to *Oxherding Tale*'s slave/son Andrew's tutelage:

> Though a slaveholder, Reverend Chandler hated slavery. He'd inherited my brother and me from his father and, out of Christian guilt, taught us more than some white men in Makanda knew, then finally released us one by one. (9)

On his deathbed, Master Chandler not only frees Rutherford and his brother, but tells his brother, "Whatever you want for you and Rutherford is yours. Tell me how you wish to be rewarded and I shall see that you have it" (116). Given that Chandler is "the most reluctant slave owner in North America," one might well ask how relevant Rutherford's experience is to understanding the general functioning and consequences of slavery. But, as in his other fiction dealing with slavery, Johnson draws universalizing conclusions about slavery and race from a "best case" slavery scenario.

Because Rutherford does not yet appreciate the "unity of Being," he resists Chandler's potentially enriching influence.[22] On the slave ship, however, Rutherford finds a more seductive surrogate White father: Captain Falcon, a "man known for his daring exploits and subjugation of the colored races from Africa to the West Indies" (29). Rutherford recognizes Falcon as an enemy, but nevertheless appreciates what he calls Falcon's "brilliance" and ultimately pities him for his human failings. Even when Falcon says, "I don't like Negroes," Rutherford has a favorable reaction: "He was frank; I liked that. With bigots a man knew where he stood" (30). It therefore comes as no surprise that Rutherford listens patiently on those occasions when Johnson uses Falcon as a mouthpiece for conservative positions on race. Falcon, for example, disparages the Nineteenth Century equivalent of affirmative action:

> I believe in *excellence*—an unfashionable thing these days, I know, what with headmasters giving illiterate Negroes degrees because they feel too guilty to fail them, then employers giving that same boy a place in the firm since he's got the degree in hand and saying no will bring a gang of Abolitionists down on their necks...Eighty percent of the crews on other ships, damn near anywhere in America, are *incompetent*, and all because everyone's ready to lower standards of excellence to make up for slavery, or discrimination, and the problem...the *problem*, Mr. Calhoun, is, I say, that most of these minorities aren't ready for the titles of quartermaster or first mate precisely because discrimination denied them the training that makes for true excellence—ready to be mediocre mates, I'll grant you that, or middlebrow functionaries, or run-of-the-mill employees, but not to *advance* the position or make a lasting breakthrough of any kind. O, 'tis a scandal on the ships I've seen, and hardly the fault of the poor half-trained Negro who hungers like anyone else these days for the glamour of titles and position. (31-2)

In response to this harangue, Rutherford apprises the reader, "though it troubles me to tell you this, I almost saw his point."

Rutherford quickly retreats from this sympathetic stance; but not, however, because he sees the racism and false logic of Falcon's position, but because of Falcon's next comment: "Now that I think of it, you remind me of a colored cabin boy named Fortunata who was aboard on my first trip to Madagascar" (32). Rutherford, who has just witnessed the emergence of a raped White cabin boy from Falcon's quarters, fears he may be next. It is thus fear of homosexual violation that distances Rutherford at this moment from Falcon, not any difference of opinion on race matters. But even though he fears becoming "Captain Ebenezer Falcon's shipboard bride," when Falcon puts a ring on Rutherford's finger, he does not rebel. Rutherford reports:

> I leaned over him, wanting to empty into his head the pistol he'd given me, but found myself transfixed by the crude ring twinned on his left hand and mine, as if, heaven help me, we were married, and the very thing I'd escaped in New Orleans had, here off the unlighted coast of Senegambia, overtaken me. (58)

As in "The Education of Mingo," the protagonist of *Middle Passage* dodges marriage with a woman, only to find himself, not entirely unhappily, "married" to a man of a different race.

Falcon further tells Rutherford that the Madagascarian cabin boy was subsequently cannibalized, adding to Rutherford's fear. But in the end, neither Falcon's position on race, nor his threat of rape or even cannibalism prevents Rutherford from identifying with him. He reports:

> I saw something—or thought I did—of myself in him and hated that. Cannibalism at sea was common enough, I knew, but he *enjoyed* telling this tale—enjoyed, as I did, any experience that disrupted the fragile, artificial pattern of life on land...above all else did Captain Falcon and his species of world conquerors thrive upon: the desire to be fascinating objects in the eyes of others. (33)

Rutherford claims to have a similar relationship with the other crew members, identifying with their positions in life, despite the fact that they are White and he is a Black man from the Antebellum South:

> We'd all blundered, failed at bourgeois life in one way or another—we were, to tell the truth, all refugees from responsibility and, like social misfits ever pushing westward to escape citified life, took to the sea as the last frontier that welcomed miscreants, dreamers, and fools. (39-40)

Later, Rutherford attempts a direct analogy between the White crew and Black slaves:

I realized, under the sun-blackened brows of slaves: men and women who had no more at stake in the fields they worked than these men in the profits of a ship owned by financiers as far away from the dangers at sea as masters from the rows of cotton their bondmen picked. No less than the blacks in the hold these sea-toughened killbucks were chattel. (87)

Much as in Johnson's other fiction, the narrator of *Middle Passage* desires to transcend the racial distinctions which have been constructed in the United States—a desire which might be seen as understandable, considering the slaughter which has been carried out in the name of race. But, as always, Johnson's alternatives to race-conscious thinking have relevance to, and thus value for, only the rarest, most privileged, lightest-skinned, Black men, and virtually no Black women. Johnson does not attempt to conceal this limitation of the vision in the novel. Except for brother Jackson (who appears only in flashback), no other Black characters in the novel share or benefit from Allmuserian phenomenology. The Allmuseri, with the exception of the virtually mute child, Baleka, are dead at the end of the novel. As for Isadora, although Johnson suggests that Rutherford's new, selfless outlook on life allows him finally to accept her love, Johnson predicates this acceptance on her having "lost about fifty pounds," her having started wearing make-up, and her willingness to finally have pre-marital sex with him. The only other major Black character in the novel is Papa Zeringue, "a man who owns half the city, has underworld connections everywhere, and kills people for interrupting him" (196). One of the plot's major developments involves the revelation that the Black crime lord owns a one-third interest in the slaveship. While Zeringue justifies his shocking participation in the slave trade by arguing for larger group financial uplift, the effect of this revelation is partially to absolve Whites of responsibility for the slave trade.

Perhaps, then, *Middle Passage* is Johnson's greatest accomplishment, for it certainly brings to full fruition a vision of life in which racial restrictions on Black men can be transcended by an effort of thought, and in which sexual divisions can only be tolerated through idealized, traditional heterosexual pairings. When one examines the ways in which this vision can be appropriated by reactionary cultural forces, it becomes imperative to step back from the type of broad celebration carried out so far in the criticism of Johnson's fiction. At a time when it may be true that few contemporary Black male writers make the bestseller list or are read in college courses, White critics should interrogate the implications of strongly critiquing a rare example of celebrated Black male writing. But to criticize some aspects of Johnson's work does not impugn it in its totality, nor does it indict contemporary Black male writers as a whole. The fact is that Johnson's work has found a place in some contemporary conservative discourse, whether he intended it to or not. In its sexist vision, Johnson's work, at best, romanticizes traditional male and female gender roles; at worst, it demonizes women. And in its revisionary representation of historical Black experience and Black/White relations, Johnson adds an African American voice to the hegemonic bloc claiming that racial discrimination is simply the result of "bad logic" on the part of White and Black individuals, and can be therefore simply thought away. In his *Los Angeles Times* review of *Middle Passage*, Arend Flick exemplifies the problematic way Johnson's texts can be used. He praises Johnson for the novel's "remarkably generous thesis":

> racism generally, and the institution of slavery in particular, might best be seen as having arisen not from political or sociological or economic causes, not (God help us) from pigment envy, but from a deep fissure that characterizes Western thought in general, our tendency to split the world into competing categories: matter and spirit, subject and object, good and evil, black and white.[24]

Flick's addition of "Western" to Johnson's more universalizing claim about human thought opens a potentially progressive space in Johnson's philosophy, but in praising Johnson's Allmuserian solution, Flick falls back into a position so abstract as to be meaningless, if not antithetical to antiracist political struggle:

> The Allmuseri become Rutherford's vehicle for self-knowledge, providing him with a passage beyond categories, beyond opposites, beyond desire and fear, and toward what we would want for him, and for ourselves. (7)

The pathos of Flick's statement is undeniable, but it ultimately participates in a dangerous ideology which blames the thinking of Black Americans for the material inequities they have always faced in the United States. It is simply untrue that slaves could pass out of slavery by attaining self-knowledge, that they could escape from a slavecatcher or a lynching mob by renouncing the "Self." Likewise, contemporary African Americans cannot create jobs and opportunities out of Buddhist, Allmuserian, phenomenological, martial arts, or any other style of transcendental thinking. As Johnson demonstrates clearly in his fiction, these practices are beneficial only to those African Americans who already have escaped the most serious material and physical hazards of racism.

As for women, the fact that in all of Johnson's critical writing he fails favorably to cite even one piece of women's writing places his work firmly in a patriarchal tradition which actively excludes women. Furthermore, his fiction, when it doesn't outright murder women, perpetuates an insistence on misogynistic standards of beauty and sexist limitations on the occupations and behavior of women. So when so much African American writing is now being published and so many Black male writers are producing remarkable work, it is appropriate to interrogate the current, near ubiquitous critical celebration of Charles Johnson's fiction.

Notes

1. Valerie Smith, "Gender and Afro-Americanist Literary Theory and Criticism," in *Speaking of Gender*, ed. Elaine Showalter, (New York: Routledge, 1989), 68.
2. bell hooks, "Reflections on Race and Sex," in *Yearning: Race, Gender, and Cultural Politics*, (Boston: South End Press, 1990), 67.
3. Sherley Anne Williams, "Some Implications of Womanist Theory," in *Reading Black, Reading Feminist*, ed. Henry Louis Gates, Jr., (New York: Meridian, 1990), 74.
4. Charles Johnson, *Being and Race: Black Writing Since 1970* (Bloomington: Indiana University Press, 1988). Further references are cited in the text.
5. An exception is Jerry W. Ward, Jr.'s review in *Callaloo*.
6. Tom LeClair, review of *Being and Race*, in *American Literature* 61 (March 1989): 135.
7. In his introduction to the 1995 reissue of *Oxherding Tale*, Johnson renews his attack on Walker, this time in staking his own novel's claim to greatness:
   Oxherding Tale appeared the same year as Alice Walker's The Color Purple. I leave it to readers to decide which book pushes harder at the boundary of invention, and inhabits most confidently the space where fiction and philosophy meet. (Charles Johnson, Oxherding Tale (NY: Plume, 1995), xviii)
8. Norman Harris, review of *Being and Race*, in *Modern Fiction Studies* 35 (Summer 1989): 308.
9. Ashraf H. A. Rushdy, "The Phenomenology of the Allmuseri: Charles Johnson and the Subject of the Narrative of Slavery," *African American Review* 26.3 (Fall 1992): 374. Further references are cited in the text.
10. It should be noted, however, that Baldwin's and Baker's "Calibans" differ greatly from Johnson's in the former writers' insistence that the dilemma cannot be transcended, that the experience of racist subordination always figures in texts by African Americans whether they acknowledge it or not. Johnson's idealistic, phenomenological "solution," on the other hand, purports to transcend this dilemma.
11. Charles Johnson, "Philosophy and Black Fiction," *Obsidian*, 6.1-2 (1980): 56-7.
12. Jacques Derrida's deconstruction of Husserl's work is probably most familiar in this respect. The Harris review cited earlier brings such questions directly to bear on Johnson's study. Harris writes:
    The most striking aspect of Johnson's formulations about the world is that it is somehow possible to be born again. And I choose the phrase "born again" because, to my knowledge, the kind of setting aside of prejudices and stripping away of artifice in order to experience what an artistic product has to offer is not supported by any "science." Indeed, if anything, philosophy and science suggest that being, or reality, is an

intermittent phenomenon, the meanings of which are contingent on any number of shifting patterns. (307)
13. William Gleason, "The Liberation of Perception: Charles Johnson's *Oxherding Tale*," in *African American Review* 25.4 (Winter 1991): 705.
14. This is, however, only a small part of this article's problems. The ungrammatical shift from the neuter pronoun to the male gendered pronoun in the above quote ("*no one* can completely divest *him*self of, well, *his* self") sends up the flag of sexual bias at the very center of a claim to universalized undifferentiated Zen experience. Indeed, throughout Johnson's fiction, as I will demonstrate below, only male characters undergo the experience of "selflessness."
15. Jennifer Hayward, "Something to Serve: Constructs of the Feminine in Charles Johnson's *Oxherding Tale*," *African American Review* 25.4 (Winter 1991): 689. Further references are cited in the text.
16. Charles Johnson, *Oxherding Tale* (New York: Grove Weidenfeld, 1982), 6. Further references are cited in the text.
17. Johnson mitigates the violence of the scene by casting it as a comic mistake on Anna's part. Unfortunately, by similarly characterizing Master Polkinghorne's rape of George's wife, Mattie, as part of a parallel "wife-swapping trick," he obscures its status as an act of slave rape. The impossibility of rendering the latter scene comic does, however, preclude Johnson from actually representing Mattie's rape; we only hear her scream.
18. Toni Morrison provides a considerable contrast to Johnson's rendering of the rape of male slaves—more realistically, by White men—in her novel, *Beloved* (New York: Alfred A. Knopf, 1987), 107-8.
19. As I end my review of the recent critical work on Johnson, I should note that the reluctance to critique him extends beyond articles in *African American Review*. Johnathan Little's "Charles Johnson's Revolutionary *Oxherding Tale*" (in *Studies in American Fiction* 19.2 (Autumn 1991): 141), for example, places the novel at the vanguard of African American fiction dealing with interracial romance, reporting that it "signals the latest and most revolutionary stage of an evolving and important literary tradition" (141). Little describes *Oxherding Tale* as "a fictive enactment of Johnson's critical expectations and criteria" (147), but, like the critics above, he fails to interrogate the politics of Johnson's non-fiction. He praises Andrew's wife's implausible "easy acceptance" of the news that her husband is "a runaway slave and part African" (146); he blames Andrew's father's death on "paranoia and obsessive racial pride," even though he is actually killed by a slavecatcher (145); and, while he argues that it is Andrew's light skin and "White" features and manner which allow him to "take on new identities and keep his mind open to the evolving and ever enriching flux of experience," he then holds him up to African Americans, including those who cannot or do not wish to pass for White, as a model for overcoming racism. While these readings are consistent with Johnson's understanding of race, their considerably problematic, if not irrational, character demands that they be interrogated.

20. Charles Johnson, *The Sorcerer's Apprentice and Other Stories* (New York: Atheneum, 1986), 105-6. Further references cited in the text.
21. Charles Johnson, *Middle Passage* (New York: Plume, 1990), 1. Further references are cited in the text.
22. Similarly, Rutherford fails to appreciate his brother Jackson's Allmuseriesque philosophy. A Saint Francis figure for whom wild birds willingly act as a cushion (Johnson reports that "they would let him lie down upon them—he was so gentle, so self-emptied" (112)), and at whose blink, flowers "explode into bloom," Jackson is Rutherford's earliest model of Johnson-style self-renunciation. Jackson turns down Master Chandler's deathbed generosity, claiming that one cannot truly own material objects, and his altruism extends to both Whites and Blacks, for he believes "it possible to serve his people by being there when they needed him—whites too, if they weren't too evil" (113). Unluckily, Rutherford appreciates the truth and beauty of his brother's philosophy of self-denial only after his terrible adventures on the slave ship.
23. Johnson's recent interview in *Contemporary Literature* suggests that his relationship with conservative thought may not be an example of unwilled textual appropriation. Besides exhibiting some of the problematic elements I noted in his earlier critical writing, such as the aesthetic dismissal of Black women's writing, in this interview Johnson cites conservative writers such as Allan Bloom and Dinesh D'Souza with approval.
24. Arend Flick, *Los Angeles Times Book Review*, 24 June 1990, 1.

CHAPTER FOUR

"Hey, Mr. Liberace, Will You Vote For Zeta?":
Looking for the *Joto* in Chicano Men's Autobiographical Writing

In exploring the North American roots of contemporary notions of *machismo*, folklorist Américo Paredes turns to "the novelist Ernest Hemingway—the most hallowed interpreter of the *macho*." Paredes notes:

> Today Hemingway is scorned by the critics. This is not surprising, since the protagonist of the novels now acclaimed by the critics no longer is the *macho* but the homosexual—the other extreme, or perhaps the same thing seen from another point of view.[1]

By placing male homosexuality on a continuum with the hypermasculine *macho*, Paredes offers a radical challenge to an understanding of male homosexuality as antithetical to masculinity. While such radicality typifies Paredes' work in the fields of folklore (his groundbreaking study, "*With His Pistol in His Hand*") and fiction (especially the "discovered" novel, *George Washington Gomez*), Paredes' insights into the relationship between homosexuality and masculinity in the contemporary novel may have been enabled in part by the prominence of male homosexuality in the few Chicano novels published at the time Paredes was composing this essay.

In 1967, modern Chicano literature only possessed, according to some definitions, two novels: Jose Antonio Villareal's *Pocho* (1959) and John Rechy's *City of Night* (1963), both of which address male homosexuality affirmatively. The latter is arguably the most celebrated gay novel in U.S. history, but even Villareal's rather conservative *bildungsroman* includes the protagonist, Richard Rubio's plea for the tolerance of homosexuals. He tells his homophobic friend:

> those two guys you were talking about—they're queer, and they have a bunch of friends that are the same way, but they're real intelligent and good people. They just happen to be like that, that's all. Like a guy with only one leg, or a deaf-and-dumb guy, or a guy with the con. They

can't help it, but they make the most of their life. And, another thing—they like being that way, and they never fool with me, because they know I'm straight, and I respect them for that. Those two guys live together, and they really love each other. You ought to see them, how nice they talk to each other and the way they take care of one another. Hell, even married people don't act that good.[2]

While a simplistic comparison of gay men to the disabled won't pass today's politically correct muster, Richard's speech has a certain radicalism, particularly in marking gay couples, in at least one important respect, more favorably than heterosexual ones.

In his pioneering article, "Homosexuality and Chicano Literature," Juan Bruce-Novoa notes this peculiar passage as well as many other representations of homosexuality in *Pocho*. He further observes that "of the seven novels published during the decade of Chicano Movement (1959-1970), five gave central importance to homosexuality."[3] Bruce-Novoa sees the recurrent, and generally favorable representations of male homosexuality in Chicano literature as a promising sign of the gender politics of the Chicano community:

> What is heartening is that in the majority of cases, homosexuals and homosexual acts are not subjected to stereotypical prejudice. If the novel gives us an accurate reading of the Chicano community—a question in itself debatable—we can say that our community is less sexually repressive than we might expect. If nothing else, among Chicano novelists there are varying attitudes and a willingness to address the topic. This makes the Chicano novel a progressive space of dialogue, an appropriate space in and through which a more androgynous and humane Chicano identity may be forged.[4]

Unfortunately, other Chicano literary critics have not approached the study of Chicano male homosexuality with Bruce-Novoa's interest or generosity.

Raymund Paredes' 1982 article, "The Evolution of Chicano Literature," for example, argues against the inclusion of John Rechy's fiction in the Chicano literary canon. He writes, "John Rechy's essay 'El Paso del Norte' certainly should be considered Chicano literature, but his novel *City of Night*, which is virtually devoid of ethnic content, probably should not."[5] Paredes does not clarify what he means by "ethnic content," and in an article published eleven years later, he expands on this exclusionary gesture, arguing that Rechy "has generally dissociated homosexual and Chicano themes in his work, primarily addressing the former in a series of well-known novels, especially *City of Night* (1963), and the latter in magazine articles and essays."[6] Recent work on Rechy, however, has challenged such easy divisions, arguing that the "homosexual theme" in Rechy's novels is deeply marked by race.[7]

As for the general status of male homosexuality in Chicano literature, Paredes writes:

> Perhaps because of the persistence of machismo and the particular pressures it brings to bear on Mexican-American men, male homosexuality, as a significant component of Chicano writing, has had a less visible impact than lesbianism...The late Arturo Islas engaged homosexuality obliquely in *The Rain God* (1984) while Richard Rodriguez hints at the issue in *Hunger of Memory*. Michael Nava has created a gay Chicano lawyer, Henry Rios, in his detective fiction, but in *Goldenboy* (1988), for example, Rios inhabits the novel as a Chicano in name only; there is no significant presentation of Chicano culture and no supporting Chicano characters...Male homosexuality is clearly an important component in contemporary Chicano writing but, unlike lesbianism, it awaits explicit and sustained engagement within the context of Mexican-American culture. (47-8)

Paredes' statement about Chicano literature's relationship to male homosexuality is confusing. While echoing Bruce-Novoa in asserting that "male homosexuality is clearly an important component in contemporary Chicano writing," Paredes nevertheless suggests that it somehow lacks "visibility," such as that achieved by lesbianism.

Even if one leaves aside Rechy and Villareal, the writers whom Paredes cites present homosexuality in a manner that is hardly invisible. Far from "oblique," homosexual characters dominate Islas' *The Rain God*, from the novel's gay protagonist to its titular secondary character, who is slain by a gaybasher.[8] Likewise, while it could be argued that Nava's *Goldenboy* does not represent gay issues "within the context of Mexican-American culture" (I would not so argue), two of Nava's subsequent Henry Rios novels deal centrally with Rios' relationship to the Chicano community: in *How Town*, Rios returns to his California Central Valley hometown to solve a crime and face his homophobic and Chicano roots, while *The Hidden Law* concerns Rios' defense of a Chicano youth for the murder of a Chicano politician. Paredes' insistence on seeing male homosexuality in a deraced manner in the face of how these novels interweave ethnic/racial and sexual representations suggests a sexual critical blindness or bias in his approach. Such a bias, it must be added, cannot originate in a respectful acknowledgement of positional difference or lack of experiential authority, since Paredes speaks freely on lesbian and other Chicana writings, literature with which he can claim no greater positional identification.

The critical sidestepping of male homosexuality appears in the major work of another prominent Chicano literary historian. In *Chicano Narrative: The Dialectics of Difference*, Ramón Saldívar admits the importance within Chicano literature of male "sexual orientation" (a code word here for homosexuality), but he likewise defers discussing it:

> While the tracing out of the gaps and silences in Chicano texts concerning men's sexual orientation, their sense of gender roles, and their oppression of women is a subject demanding a book-length analysis in

its own right, I have tried to sketch out the preliminary borders of that theoretical terrain within a race and class analysis of Chicano writings.⁹

Like Paredes, Saldívar claims to support the examination of male (homo)sexuality in Chicano literature, but politely bows out of doing it himself, even though he does not have a similar reluctance to speak on Chicana writing, lesbian or heterosexual.

A third example—Carl Gutiérrez-Jones' 1995 study, *Rethinking the Borderlands Between Chicano Culture and Legal Discourse*—helps open my own commentary on Chicano writing. In the context of examining the relationship of legal experience and discourse to Chicano cultural production, Gutiérrez-Jones discusses the way that male/male bonds consolidate patriarchal power. Drawing on the work of Eve Kosofsky Sedgwick, Gutiérrez-Jones writes, "Assumptions about sexuality and, at certain historical junctures, sexual identity are...mobilized in ways that best benefit the historically specific needs of the patriarchal moment."¹⁰ Making astute use of Sedgwick's theories, Gutiérrez-Jones demonstrates how *The Revolt of the Cockroach People*, the second of Oscar Zeta Acosta's two autobiographical novels, participates in the homosocial reinforcement of patriarchal privilege.

Gutiérrez-Jones notes that the social upheavals of the 1960's threatened Chicano male privilege and also shaped the strategies Chicano men deployed to maintain that privilege. He adds that among those strategies, "one of the more volatile yet 'effective' included defining the Chicano community as a social group consensually unified around a reverence for machismo" (134). Gutiérrez-Jones documents Acosta's participation in this strategy, noting, for example, that "in a legal position paper, Acosta made machismo the fundamental motor behind Chicano interaction" (134). Even if the trope of machismo successfully condensed a discourse of Chicano identity which brought Chicanas and Chicanos together in a way which helped them resist White domination, its effectiveness, Gutiérrez-Jones argues, was severely impaired in many respects, foremost of which was the maintenance of the traditional subordination of Chicanas.

The kind of machismo which Acosta mobilizes also has a strategic weakness related to the participation of a racist legal system in its condensation. Through a reading of Acosta's novel and Edward James Olmos' film *American Me*, Gutiérrez-Jones demonstrates how "the patriarchal imperatives of both U.S. legal culture and Chicano culture have collaborated in the codification of machismo as a concept around which to ground cultural affiliation" (124). Gutiérrez-Jones goes on, however, to suggest that, rather than a mere convergence of Chicano patriarchal and racist legal interests, machismo actually emerges as an almost unilateral imposition of White power. Machismo, he writes, is:

> a form of masculine bonding best understood not as a "natural" or inevitable cultural factor unifying Chicano communities but rather as

a replication, albeit culturally influenced, of social conventions embedded in, and perpetuated by, the law. (123-4)

Gutiérrez-Jones illustrates the dangers of the racist involvement of the law, showing how the kind of machismo fostered by the U.S. legal system engenders internecine Chicano male struggles for power: "the law promulgates homosocial bonds in such a way as to limit revolutionary actions by setting marginalized groups into patterns of self-inflicted violence" (133).

Gutiérrez-Jones demonstrates that even though Acosta's two novels point to the dangers of this kind of machismo, Acosta refuses to critique masculinist anti-racist strategies. Gutiérrez-Jones writes:

> While it appears that Acosta...considers the more general patterns of self-inflicted violence a central problem for Chicanos, one linked to the manipulations of hegemony, [he] demonstrate[s] a tendency to deflect such gender and sexuality issues when the homosocial register could be approached more critically. (133)

A Sedgwickian critique of homosocial power structures, Gutiérrez-Jones suggests, could help expose the disabling participation of White supremacist interests in certain constructions of machismo, and, subsequently, in larger constructions of Chicano identity. Sedgwick's concepts and terminology thus provide a means for Gutiérrez-Jones to critique the sexist Achilles' heel of Acosta's machismo-based anti-racist strategy.

Unfortunately, Gutiérrez-Jones' particular use of Sedgwick's work also has the effect of eliding the homosexual content of Acosta's novel.[11] Gutiérrez-Jones' use of Sedgwick's analytical tools organizes the terrain of male/male relationships so as to render any serious consideration of male homosexuality impossible. Explaining the structure of the male homosocial continuum, Gutiérrez-Jones writes:

> What may be mistakenly considered in the contemporary context as "sexual givens"—primarily the distinction between heterosexuality and homosexuality—in turn need to be recognized as provisional sociocultural negotiations that guarantee particular privileges and rights to particular males. (132)

Much lesbian/gay political struggle, however, works exactly toward societal acceptance of homosexuality as a "given," since, at least in the short term, heterosexuality is unlikely to be de-naturalized. The understanding of homosexuality as contingent alongside a natural heterosexuality is one of lesbian and gay people's biggest political and conceptual obstacles. Attempts to subsume homosexuality within other social processes must therefore be approached carefully. Thus, while Gutiérrez-Jones' historicization of the concept of homo/heterosexuality is sound, his reading of Acosta's novel has limited value for a queer politics, for it denies the possibility of homosexuality as anything other than a psychic threat controlling men within patriarchy. Gutiérrez-Jones cites Sedgwick in his refusal to read homosexuality in the Chicanos of Acosta's novel:

> To claim, then, that homosocial bonding significantly informs a particular group's relations—for instance, Chicano nationalist relations described in Acosta's novel—is not the same as to argue that such a group is latently homosexual. Instead, Sedgwick leads us beyond the artificial binary between homosexual and heterosexual orientations, demonstrating how they give way to a more complex continuum of desires. (133)

My reading of Acosta, on the other hand, resists moving "beyond" homosexuality; it refuses to grant any homosocial "continuum of desires" a more complex, less "artificial" character than homosexual desire. Sedgwick's own work, while arguing the importance of seeing the connection of male/male desire to patriarchy, does not deny the sexual character of much male/male desire. In the reading which follows, I look at/for homosexuality by exploring Acosta's peculiar rendering of the heterosexual desire of the narrator of his two autobiographical novels, raising in the process (as crass as it may be) the possibility that his memoirs are, at least in part, the product of a homosexual closet. Finally, in examining the process by which such a closet might be maintained, I hope to demonstrate the way one discourse of identity–here specifically racial–can be deployed in the service of another.

Acosta's two autobiographical novels refer obsessively to homosexuality. Unfortunately, as Bruce-Novoa notes, his "references to gays become leitmotif of negative signification," adding that as Acosta's two volumes progress, the homophobia becomes more pronounced:

> At the start Acosta depicts himself as a liberal, sexually tolerant lawyer, yet "faggot" becomes his supreme insult. At first it is lightly despetivo, meaning old or boring, but by the end of Brown Buffalo Acosta groups homosexuals with society's dregs, using guilt by association: "winos and fags" (197). The negative synonymy is even more pronounced in *Cockroach*, where homosexual and enemy result [sic] synonyms...homosexuality signifies the evil other, the inhuman, the trace of condemnation. Despite Acosta's obvious satiric intent in every facet of his texts, the homophobia is still offensive.[12]

Bruce-Novoa accurately characterizes the trajectory of homophobia through the two novels (although I find the homophobia strong, even from the beginning). Gutiérrez-Jones likewise notes the strong homophobia of Acosta's second text, noting that in *The Revolt of the Cockroach People* "homosexual association is consistently used as a sign of derision" (137).

Sedgwick's insights help make sense, however, of the coexistence of such homophobia with the clear affiliation the narrator feels with lesbian and gay people. In what follows, I examine three areas which involve the narrator in homosexuality: his undisguised fraternization with and fondness for homosexual characters; his haunting by an eroticized paranoid male double; and, finally, the varied yet persistent deferral of the narrator's heterosexual activity in the face of his self-proclaimed hyperactive heterosexuality.

A number of the narrator's more famous acquaintances are, in the narrator's ubiquitous term, "fags." He recalls friendship, for example, with Timothy Leary, "the old fag"[13] and with Van Tilburg Clark, Mark Harris, Herb Gold, "the world famous fags" (100).[14] Homosexual celebrities do not need to be alive in order for the narrator to identify with them. At one point, seeing himself in a barroom mirror, the narrator reflects, "I am the son of Lorca, I remind myself. The only poet of this century worth reading. Did he suffer with those black eyes? That smooth, long greaser hair; did it make him hurt?" (67). Lorca's homosexuality does not forestall the narrator's rather sensual identification with him, significantly his only identification with a twentieth century poet.[15] Similarly, the narrator's sole Chicano friend ("Jose, [the] only countryman I'd known in San Francisco" (50)) is a gay artist.[16]

Aside from these affirmative identifications, the narrator encounters a remarkable number of other gay and lesbian characters in his travels. He characterizes his Boy Scout leader John Hazard as a "fag"; he describes his psychiatrist Dr. Serbin as "that skinny fag without character" (14). The narrator claims that he doesn't "give a shit about [the] sex life" of "fag" pizza parlor owner Cheto Connetto (145).[17] As for women, the narrator counts among his friends at JJ's "Maria, the Jewish switchhitter [who would] occasionally hustle whatever strangers—male or female—happened to drop in" (44). The narrator expresses no discomfort when he and Maria "drove over to Sausalito and got drunk at the No Name Bar with some fag friends of hers" (46). Even a three month relationship—his "only serious affair of the sixties" (47)—is with a woman rumored to have "lesbian problems" (52).

An observation near the end of *The Autobiography of a Brown Buffalo* adds a final oblique moment of identification (one which, as noted above, Bruce-Novoa reads differently as homophobic). In the midst of his growing self-insight in Mexico, the narrator notices the effect of rain on the people at a plaza:

> The winos and the fags are the last to leave the benches beside the water fountains spouting water. I walk alone on the sidewalks with the rain smacking my face. I look up, open my mouth and drink. (197-8)

Once it begins to rain, the narrator remains with the winos and, more importantly for my reading, the "fags." The syntagmatic representation of winos/fags/me articulates a connection which belies the narrator's fervent attempt to distance himself from homosexuals.[18]

A second homosexual presence in *The Autobiography of a Brown Buffalo* involves the narrator's relationship to his "fag" analyst, Dr. Serbin. The novel opens with the narrator's naked self-examination. After a thorough assessment of his body, he attempts to vomit, but is interrupted by "that faint voice of Dr. Serbin." The narrator notes, "Lately Dr. Serbin has taken to following me wherever I go" (13). One can interpret the imaginary presence of the Jewish psychiatrist in numerous ways. Joe E. Rodriguez argues that "The therapist represents 'Oscar's' need to integrate different aspects of his personality and find a measure of inner peace."[19] For the purposes of this chapter, however, I pursue a homosocial/-sexual interpretation of the relationship.

Sedgwick's important work on the sexual character of Gothic male doubles makes it difficult to avoid considering a sexual reading of the narrator's psychological possession, particularly since he repeatedly identifies Serbin as a "fag." Sedgwick characterizes works such as *Frankenstein*, *Caleb Williams* and *Confessions of a Justified Sinner* as Gothic novels "about one or more males who not only is persecuted by, but considers himself transparent to and often under the compulsion of, another male."[20] Sedgwick suggests that we can "follow Freud in hypothesizing that such a sense of persecution represents the fearful, phantasmic rejection by recasting of an original homosexual (or even merely homosocial) desire."[21] Sedgwick opens the possibility that the paranoid male double in Gothic fiction can not only stand as a mark of homosocial control, but (and this is where her work departs from Gutiérrez-Jones) also as a sign of repressed homosexuality. It is in this spirit of pluralistic interpretive modes that I want to think about Acosta's doubles.

The narrator reports, "Ever since he took to following me I've found it rather difficult to ignore him" (14). More interesting than Dr. Serbin's ubiquity, however, are the psychiatrist's frequent bodily intrusions. Not only does he appear in the narrator's car and office, he shows up in the most private places, at the most improper times, from the bathroom incident noted above and a toilet stall at work to the shower while the narrator masturbates.[22] The narrator reports that, just as "the brown giant explodes...The fucking shrink steps into the shower and says, 'Did you ever stop to consider that it might simply be a form of self-love'" (16). Dr. Serbin's observation of the narrator's masturbatory life is, in fact, a regular occurrence. The narrator pleads to the reader:

> Can you understand what it feels like to wake up late at night with only the sounds of cable cars jerking along Hyde and foghorns down the street at Aquatic Park? There you are, staring hot-eyed at the ceiling, the beast in your anxious hand in the darkness of the night sweating over some hot fantasy you want to stab before she gets away and suddenly you hear him breathing quietly, observing you from his chair and saying something cute like, 'Who do you think she is?' (14)

Dr. Serbin's interruptions of the narrator's masturbation become so troublesome that he tries to escape observation through the use of drugs:

> what I usually do when I catch him in my room interrupting my fantasies, I simply take another of those green jobs with chloroform, rip me off a piece, lay back and wait for the clock hand to turn. (15)

Acosta clearly is parodying psycho-sexual analytic rhetoric in his treatment of Dr. Serbin. Even the narrator is in on the joke, commenting at one point, for instance, "I especially like it when he says, 'That really wasn't Alice you strangled in the bathtub. It was her boyfriend, Ted'" (14). Dr. Serbin's sexualized haunting, however, takes on a less parodic tone when the narrator finally gets the courage to break from him. Acosta describes the narrator's joy in language scarcely touched by parody:

> I cannot control myself. The laughter of madness clenches my throat. Tears are flowing down my fat cheeks, their wetness is warm. A ghost shivers down my back. But I feel good. I shake it off and go to seek more of that demon rum. There is nothing to stop me now. I have paid all my debts, I have paid all my dues and now nothing remains but the joy of madness. Another wild Indian gone amok. (42)

Rejecting Serbin and his paranoid double gives the narrator's sex life a jump start; that evening he has sex with a woman for the first time in over a year, prompting him to reflect, "I should fire my shrink more often" (65). Dr. Serbin largely disappears at this point in the novel, reappearing only a few more times.[23] An interpretation of Dr. Serbin as something more than a parody of psychoanalysis, however, finds further evidence in the proliferation of other, less ghostly male voyeurs participating in the narrator's sex life, from a male friend's instruction in masturbation to his first experience with prostitution.

While he is a teenager, the narrator's friends spy on him, after an elaborate trick to convince him to have sex with a prostitute:

> I had already finished twice when I heard a giggle. I looked between my legs as I lay on my back, with Ruby on her knees above me, and I saw Dragalong peering through a curtain of colored beads which led into the kitchen. "Go to it, Oscar! Give it to her again!" (111)

This scene reflects the homosocial male coercion as well as the voyeuristic homosexual/social component of some kinds of public heterosexual male display.[24]

A parallel situation in *The Revolt of the Cockroach People* echoes and expands on the homosexual/social potential of this scene. In Acapulco, two prostitutes suggest a group sex encounter with the narrator and his twin brother (of whom, significantly, there is no mention in the first novel). The narrator doesn't accept the offer, but nonetheless ends up with another man watching him have sex. As the narrator enters one of the prostitutes' room, "a man walks out of the toilet buttoning his pants":

> "He wants to know if you mind if he watches...He just wants to see us do it," Betti says.
> "What is he, some kind of pervert?"
> "No, he's just a dirty old man. He says he didn't get satisfied with Carmela...What do you think?"
> ..."Tell the man...I don't care. Just hurry and get in."
> Betti goes to the door and tells the man. He comes in and sits quietly in the corner of a low soft chair. I can hear him breathing...I hear the old man breathing in puffs in the corner. I cannot see him, I can only hear him. But I don't care anymore. I am into flesh...When it is over, the man in the white suit and the Panama hat walks out without a word. (192-4)[25]

A final sexual consideration in *The Autobiography of a Brown Buffalo*, and to a lesser extent, *The Revolt of the Cockroach People*, is the narrator's persistent deferral of heterosexual activity. In characterizing Acosta's novel as the generic form of satire, Hector Calderon cites, among other features, the narrator's "unheroic efforts with women."[26] While the narrator thematizes his sexual challenges, he does not characterize his failures as "unheroic," if that term is meant to evoke a failure of masculinity: he is courageous, or at least extraordinarily assertive in his sexual pursuit, and he could hardly declare more forcefully a commitment to heterosexuality. Instead of a gender failing, the narrator identifies racial/ethnic problems at the root of his quasi-impotence. His deferral of sex results not, he suggests, from any gendered (or individual) choice of object, but rather a racial choice. Much of the first novel concerns the narrator's struggle for affirmed Chicano identity through the rejection of White supremacist sexual desire.

Near the end of *The Autobiography of a Brown Buffalo*, the narrator recalls his "very first experience with a woman"[27]:

> she asked if I wanted to see what was under her panties. To be quite honest I had never seen even the underskirts of my various cousins' chones, so she lifted up her little red dress and I gently touched that fatty excitement which would hound me for the rest of my life. (185)

The narrator's characterization of heterosexual desire as something "hounding him" finds expression in its development as a site of intense conflict and disappointment.

The narrator's first sexual setback comes as an eleven year-old. His crush on blonde, blue-eyed Jane Addison ends with her remark in class that he smells bad. The narrator links this refection to his race, reporting:

> The room is filled with laughter. My ears pound red. I am done for. My heart sags from the overpowering weight of the fatness of my belly. I am the nigger, after all. My mother was right. I am nothing but an

> Indian with sweating body and faltering tits that sag at the sight of a young girl's blue eyes. I shall never be able to undress in front of a woman's stare. I shall refuse to play basketball for fear that some day I might have my jersey ripped from me in front of those thousands of pigtailed, blue-eyed girls from America. (94-5)

Later, he repeats, "I had been way down girl-wise ever since Jane Addison told me I stunk" (114). The narrator's painful recollection becomes the rationale not only for future limitations on traditionally masculine activity such as playing basketball, but for limitations on his sexual relationships with women, limitations which grow in number and severity.

At twelve, an experience with his cousin adds a prohibitive moral stance against sex to the racial/physical one the narrator says he already possesses:

> She was a bit younger but had already learned the ropes when she asked me if I wanted to learn the tricks of the trade. Everything was going well until we heard a knock on the door. My brother Bob hollered for us to open. We maintained and he shouted, "I know what you guys are doing. Open up!" After he left, she got right back to it. But it wouldn't expand. It wouldn't budge an inch no matter how hard we tried. She blamed it on me, naturally, and said, "You must never leave a girl with a tickle like I've got…now do it or I'll tell my dad."
>
> So for six months I refused to visit any relative, and for six months I suffered, suffocated, choked and sweated every hour of the day. I turned to God and prayed hourly. In bed, in the shower, at school, at the Boy Scout meetings, out in the orchards and in my tree house where I still maintained vigil in case the enemy broke the treaty. Everywhere and at all times I promised Him for six months that no matter what had happened, if He would keep her mouth shut, I'd save my cherry for my bride. (108)

The narrator attributes his next three years of celibacy to a holy vow: "I had made a promise to God that if my cousin didn't spill the beans on me, I'd keep that nasty thing in my pants until I married" (108). Despite his brother's confession to having satisfied his cousin's "tickle" after the narrator left her, he reaffirms his vow: "A deal is a deal, no matter what, and I had sworn to remain a virgin" (109).

While he is in high school, he has a group of friends—the Fearless Four—whose obsession is bedding women. Their success, however, does not measure up to their desire:

> I must confess that in three years of pussy-chasing the Fearless Four never made a single score…although I was first string on the football team, first soloist in the reed section of the concert and dance bands and president of my class, I never had a girlfriend and I never scored any chick in school or on the streets. (107)

At this point, the narrator adds several new entries to his expanding list of reasons for his failed heterosexuality:

> none of us could pick up a broad. Perhaps it was our reputation for being the biggest drunks in school. Or the fact the everyone knew that the real reason we called Tim Watkins Dragalong was not because of his cast, but because he had a ten inch cock, when soft. (108)

When the narrator is fifteen, three of the Fearless Four discover prostitution, but in spite of their encouragement the narrator remains pure:

> Try as they might, I had kept myself out of those private rooms for a year and a half...But, God how I itched. No one will ever know my absolute aching for just a crack at one of those hussies. Ruby was so fantastic I wouldn't dare to dream of her. But when she'd sit next to me, her dress up to her knees and her Portuguese tits hanging in front of me...Christ!...at times I almost had to forcibly restrain myself from crashing into that room and ripping her apart with my bare hands. (109)

In spite of the purported strength of his sexual desire, the narrator cannot overcome the various obstacles to his "ripping her apart." Homophobic taunts, however, quickly get him in bed.

One evening Ruby, the brothel's madame, reports that her boss has been complaining about the narrator's sexual inactivity:

> "I told him you were studying for the priesthood."
> "I'm not going to be a God damn priest, Ruby! What'd you say that for?"
> "Well, I'm sorry, dear...but he accused you of...you know, he said you were...sissy. The bastard actually tried to tell me you were a homosexual." (110)

Furious, the narrator cries, "Fuck God and fuck the Pope," and leads Ruby to her room. Although he attributes his capitulation to Ruby's desirability, her beauty overcomes his resistance only when he also comes under the suspicion of homosexuality.[28]

A year later, racism looms again as a scourge to the narrator's heterosexuality, when his first, White, girlfriend Alice's parents prohibit their relationship, forcing them to meet secretly for a year. The narrator notes, however, "I never screwed her," the reason for which he does not explain. This celibate romance continues until her parents bring in the law:

> After that, we just gave up. We made the decision to simply suffer. The day she was eighteen—four years hence—we'd get married in my mother's Catholic Church...I figured the best thing to do was to stay away from Riverbank until our wedding, and the four-year enlistment was just the thing to do. (129)

Their plans fold, however, when, a few months into his military enlistment, the narrator receives a "dear john" letter from Alice, who is marrying a White man. He reacts strongly to this rejection, and shortly afterwards turns even more forcefully to religion:

> I went to confession for the first time in five years and told the priest that I had committed a mortal sin…"I've made a…god out of my girlfriend…when I say my prayers, I see her sitting on the altar"…I did the penance but there were no miracles. I still felt guilty as sin for worshipping Alice, especially after she'd dumped me for a greasy, God damn Wop. So I started to read the Bible and go to church every night. (130-1)

His religious devotion increases after his conversion to an evangelical form of Baptism, and the effect on his sex life is considerable: "I no longer went to movies, quit playing jazz and didn't touch my penis except to piss for two whole years" (132).

The next few years of the narrator's life receive scarce attention; he reveals little details beyond the fact that he gives up religion, attempts suicide, has two nervous breakdowns and starts practicing law in San Francisco. There, his sexual misadventures continue. Recalling, for example, an attempt at a sexual liaison with his bisexual friend, Maria, which ends with him falling asleep drunk in the bathtub, he jokingly blames his impotence on "an accident" (46). Subsequently, he remarks, "Maria became one of the many women friends I always kept around to protect me from the Frisco fog and my dead vine. I never screwed any of them, I just kept them to hear me out" (46).

He similarly describes his relationship with Maryjane and Bertha, two others of those "many woman friends":

> The truth of the matter was we *were* sleeping together. Stoned drunk, late at night we'd pass out in whoever's bed happened to be handy. It boosted the hell out of my ego, but it did absolutely nothing for my abandoned lily. (52)

These two women desire him, but he cannot oblige them, offering them a different excuse: "It's those fucking pills my shrink makes me take. I just can't get it up" (64). Finally, out with Maryjane one night, he asks himself, "Why in God's name didn't I ever fuck her?" (63) and has sex with her, feeling "atingle for the first time in over a year!" (64).[29] This sexual encounter provides a kind of turning point in his sexual life by not only reaffirming his potency, but by initiating a new sexual quest the narrator links to his "becoming Chicano."

At age thirty-one the narrator is in a state of sexual dysfunction which he will come to understand in the course of the novel as the result of his sexual repudiation of Mexican women. The obstacles affecting the narrator's heterosexual performance up to this point, as I have noted, have been varied. As his consciousness of his Chicano identity begins to develop, however, he begins to subsume these various frustrations under a single problem: ethnic self-hate. Several times in his recollections the narrator addresses his never having dated Chicanas: "I didn't for twenty years. All through school, in the Air Force, in San Francisco and in Alpine, I did not know one Mexican girl that aroused the beast in me" (112). At first, he attributes his not having dated Chicanas, at least in part, to Chicanas themselves:

> I never went out with the few Mexican girls in school because they always stuck to themselves and refused to participate in the various activities...they always held back, eating their lunch under the shed for the bicycles instead of on the lawn with "the rest of the people."

He also declares them to be "square and homely" (112).

Early in *The Revolt of the Cockroach People* the narrator adds more information about his early turning away from Chicanas sexually. After he leads a revolt against the racism of his middle school's attempt to pair boys and girls in the graduation march by race instead of height as planned, the narrator incurs the wrath of the Chicanas who perceive this action as a "rejection":

> The Mexican girls never spoke to me again. Even when I became the solo clarinetist in the dance band, when I won my three stripes for varsity football, when I was elected class president, they never forgave me my rejection. (31)

Acosta's two volume autobiographical novel ultimately hangs the narrator's sexual "recovery" on mending this early rift with Chicanas.

Near the end of *The Autobiography of a Brown Buffalo*, after many travels, the narrator declares, "I decided to go to El Paso, the place of my birth, to see if I could find the object of my quest. I still wanted to find out just who in the hell I really was" (184). Having crossed into Mexico at the El Paso border, the narrator indeed finds out "who the hell he really is," and that discovery lies in an intersectional sexual/racial process.

In Juarez, he reports:

> My head was in a quagmire, twisted with the delights of the most beautiful women I'd ever seen in my life...Whatever Alice Joy or Jane Addison meant to me as a kid, now they were only grade school memories of a time gone by. I was thirty-three when I hit the streets of Juarez and I had never found a woman to love in all my travels. But that first night out on the town, I saw at least a thousand I'd have married gladly on the spot if they'd given me a tumble...My heart ached to speak with any of these women. I knew they had the answer to my pain. If I could only speak whatever language I could muster, I was certain they'd give me the cure for my ailing stomach, my ulcers and the blood in the toilet. (189)

The women who actually "cure" his stomach, and, he claims, his identity problems, are prostitutes:

> they both took me into the bedrooms behind the *Cantina de la Revolucion* where I learned how to be a serious Mexican for the first time in my life. If you want an exact date, you can say that I became a true son of the *indio* from the mountains of Durango on January 9, 1968...I felt like a man should feel when he's on the lam, on the loose in search of his fucked-up identity. (190)

Critics have not failed to pick up on the sexual nature of the narrator's racial self-discovery. Vernon E. Lattin paraphrases the narrator's self-analysis in his article, "Ethnicity and Identity in the Contemporary Chicano Novel":

> [The narrator's] reaction to being different is to try to get rid of the differences, to assimilate. To compensate for the fear of being naked in front of those "pigtailed, blue-eyed girls from America," he has sexual experiences with only Anglo girls. His quest for identity, which literally involves driving across much of America to Juarez, is a journey back in memory and time. In Juarez he sees all the beautiful brown women and begins to find himself as an individual and as a Chicano.[30]

In a more extended discussion of sexuality and internalized racism, Genaro M. Padilla details how a Chicano's attraction to White women becomes a touchstone of ethnic self-hate:

> instead of seeking a positive self-image within the context of one's own race and culture, the dark child often builds an imaginative but self-denying ideal of whiteness. With some variation, this is the labyrinthine pattern into which Acosta falls. He makes himself forget the incident [with Jane Addison] and its humiliating implications; he continues to idealize America's blue-eyed girls. Willfully self-blinded, he pursues a course which increasingly leads him away from his culture and from himself.[32]

Padilla, like Lattin, accepts in full the narrator's (hetero)sexualized version of affirming his ethnicity. Padilla writes:

> Acosta discovers himself when he achieves identification as a Chicano. It is, predictably enough, in the city of his birth, El Paso, Texas, that he finally begins to come to terms with himself and his ancestry...For the first time in his adult life, he looks upon Mexican women as life-giving and beautiful. Finally the obsession with the white goddesses of his youth is obliterated. (254)

While I do not disagree with these readings, I feel that they limit themselves by strictly accepting the narrator's account of the relationship between sexuality and ethnicity in his development, a particularly restrictive gesture since the texts offer evidence of the narrator's flipflopping on this score.[31]

I see these critics' acceptance of the narrator's sexual rationalizations as part of the critical trend I tried to sketch at the beginning of this chapter, a trend which has a hard time seeing or talking about any Chicano sexuality but heterosexuality. Regardless of what the narrator of Acosta's novels, or even Acosta himself, wanted readers to know about his sexual world, a queer reading is not only quite possible, I hope to have shown, but might help explain parts of Acosta's text which might otherwise appear to be simply "eccentric" or perhaps a result of Acosta's feverish substance abuse. I nonetheless fear that my reading might be considered simply an attempt to expose Acosta.

This is the problem with writing about the queerness of texts by authors who are not "out" as lesbian/gay people: the critic's arguments are often dismissed as violation (as in the furor over "outing"), wishful thinking, projection—any number of "self-serving" reasons. I therefore have chosen to pair my reading of Acosta's novels with a reading of Richard Rodriguez. His recent coming out as a gay man retrospectively confirms the queer identity of the closeted narrator of Rodriguez's 1982 autobiography, *Hunger of Memory*. What follows, however, is not an attempt to psychoanalyze the younger Rodriguez; instead, it is an examination, with the knowledge that Rodriguez later comes out, of the textual strategies he uses to disguise homosexuality in his autobiography, and the relationship between those strategies and his conservative positions on race.[33] Rodriguez's autobiography provides an unusually clear delineation of the "psychodynamics" of the closeted writer and of the way rhetorics of race and sex/gender structure each other in the constitution and representation of identity.

In 1982, Rodriguez published *Hunger of Memory*, his account of growing up Chicano in the United States. In the text he identifies himself as heterosexual, indicating an early shyness and insecurity around girls, but writing that by college he "began to have something like a conventional sexual life."[34] A decade later, however, in a *Los Angeles Times Magazine* critique of "conventional" notions of family, another Rodriguez emerges. In this piece, he claims a "sexual life" which many would designate as "unconventional." "I am," he states, "a homosexual Catholic."[35]

When Rodriguez came out, it undoubtedly provided a certain satisfaction to lesbian/gay readers whose "gaydar" had detected a queer in his earlier text. Cherrie Moraga, for example, notes that "even ten years ago we all knew 'Mr. Secrets' was gay from his assimilationist *Hunger of Memory*."[36] Curiously, however, those who have commented on Rodriguez's homosexuality most frequently cite the essay, "Late Victorians," from his 1993 collection, *Days of Obligation: An Argument with my Mexican Father*. Ilan Stavans, for example, writes that in "*Days of Obligation*, Richard Rodriguez includes an essay, 'Late Victorians,' about his own homosexuality and AIDS."[37] But while "Late Victorians" addresses the issues of homosexuality and AIDS, Rodriguez's relationship to these issues is only implicit; any "coming out" in this text is couched in Rodriguez's typically precious, oblique language. Parallelism is Rodriguez's trope of choice: gay men lift weights/I lift weights; gay men live in the Castro District of San Francisco/I live in the Castro District of San Francisco, etc.. Rodriguez never makes a declarative assertion of his homosexuality on the order of "I am gay."

Now it is, of course, Rodriguez's prerogative to come out in whatever manner he chooses; some doubtlessly admire the delicate aesthetic effect of his veiled revelations. What is important for my purposes, however, is that even when Rodriguez comes out, he does so in an evasive manner. One must ask why oblique gestures toward homosexual identification in "Late Victorians" are considered coming out, when equally (in)direct references to Rodriguez's homosexuality in his earlier work are not viewed as such. In other words, if both texts "reveal" Rodriguez's homosexuality, what differentiates between the two so strongly that together they can mark a rupture as ostensibly important as that between homo- and heterosexuality or between the closeted and the out?

Lack of clarity around an issue such as sexuality becomes an even more critical issue when other political/identity issues find direct expression. Despite Rodriguez's notoriously elliptical writing style, he makes many assertions, particularly regarding race and ethnicity politics, with little or no artful ambiguity. For example, in *Hunger of Memory* Rodriguez undisguisedly condemns bilingual education ("Spanish would have been a dangerous language for me to have used at the start of my education" (34)); he similarly records his opposition to affirmative action ("I continued to speak out in opposition to affirmative action. I publicly scorned the university president's call for a nonwhite leadership class" (166)). Given the clarity of these and other declarations of his political beliefs, it is imperative to interrogate political sites at which he retreats into less declarative language.

Of all the intersections operating in Rodriguez's writing, perhaps most familiar is his pitting of class concerns against anti-racist efforts. Throughout his work Rodriguez argues for the rejection of raced-based civil rights claims in favor of activism aimed at empowering the poor. Chicano scholars and activists, among others, have exposed the weakness of Rodriguez's arguments, arguing most persuasively that his simplistic either/or logic of race and class politics wrongly concludes that if class oppression is more severe than racism (a contestable claim itself) then race-based remedies to social injustice should be dropped. Such reasoning is no more logical than arguing that the body's undeniable need for oxygen precludes its need for water. Rodriguez's successful dependence on this argument nevertheless continues to this day.[38]

Rodriguez uses an analogous strategy to (mis)represent his sexuality in his autobiography. Just as he deploys class rhetoric to discredit race-based political action, he exploits racial rhetoric to defuse potential signifiers of queer sexuality. To prop up a claim of heterosexuality that the homoeroticism of his text belies, Rodriguez, perhaps surprisingly, invokes racism.[39] *Hunger of Memory*'s chapter, "Complexion" addresses, as the title coyly suggests, the subject of race, but it also contains the book's most extended discussion of his sexuality.

The second section of the chapter begins: "Complexion. My first conscious experience of sexual excitement concerns my complexion" (123). Rodriguez proceeds to detail this experience: his first conscious observation of sexual intimacy between his parents juxtaposed with his mother's warning to him to avoid tanning. The connection appears, at first blush, to be nothing more than mere contiguity of experience. The relationship between race and sexuality, of course, turns out to be more profound than merely syntactic.

As his rumination on "complexion" proceeds, Rodriguez attributes the absence of heterosexuality in his early life to racially marked feeling of ugliness. He recounts horrific tales of the internalized racism of some Chicanos (dark children called *mi feito*—"my little ugly one," home preventions for dark skin in fetuses which risk causing abortion, adults reviling the darkness of their partners, etc.). Surrounded by such attitudes and practices, Rodriguez writes, "Nothing else about my appearance would concern me so much as the fact that my complexion was dark" (125). Although Rodriguez confusingly reports, "I really didn't consider my dark skin a racial characteristic" (125), he nevertheless uses a darkskinned "inferiority complex" to explain why he did not have an active heterosexual life:

> Simply, I judged myself ugly. And, since the women in my family had been the ones who discussed it in such worried tones, I felt my dark skin made me unattractive to women. (125)

He claims that his mother and other women's condemnation of dark skin led him to grow "divorced from [his] body" (125), caused him to deny himself "a sensational life" (126). He writes, "I wanted to forget that I had a body because I had a brown body" (126).

In these passages, Rodriguez is characteristically acute at representing the abuse to which people of color are subject in a White supremacist culture. His goal, however, is not to analyze White supremacy or polemicize against it; Rodriguez articulates his feeling of racial unattractiveness to disguise his lack of sexual interest in women as the reverse—their rejection of him, something I hope to have suggested Acosta's narrator also does.[40] Thus, Rodriguez's refusal to acknowledge the racism which devastated his self esteem simultaneously is enabled by and enables the sublimation of his homosexuality.

The most powerful evidence of Rodriguez's homosexuality, however, lies in his sensuously detailed interest in working class Chicano men. Recounting his youth, Rodriguez writes:

> I would notice the shirtless construction workers, the roofers, the sweating men tarring the street in front of the house. And I'd see the Mexican gardeners. I was unwilling to admit the attraction of their lives. I tried to deny it by looking away. But what was denied became strongly desired. (126)

Rodriguez writes, "though I feared looking like them, it was with silent envy that I regarded them still. I envied them their physical lives, their freedom to violate the taboo of the sun" (126). Hearing of an opportunity to work a construction job after college, Rodriguez reports, "Desire uncoiled within me" (131). In these lines, erotic terms and phrases ("attraction," "shirtless, sweating men," "uncoiling desire") are juxtaposed with expressions of repression ("unwillingness to admit," "denial," "fear," "taboo"). To contain these signifiers of repressed homosexuality—"positive" ones even more threatening than the "negative" one of lack of interest in women—Rodriguez again turns to the rhetoric of race.

Citing his mother's warning that a dark tan makes him resemble Chicano day laborers in an undesirable way, Rodriguez reports that his fascination with these men lay in their skin color:

> I would sit forward in the back seat of our family's 48 Chevy to see them, working alongside Valley highways: dark men on an even horizon, loading a truck amid rows of straight green. Powerful, powerless men. Their fascinating darkness—like mine—to be feared. (114)

In this manner, Rodriguez articulates this "fascination" as an instance of racial identification, whereas it might otherwise be read as sexual. But while Rodriguez's racial identification allows him to conceal the sexual nature of his interest in the *braceros*, this identification is at odds with other aims of the text, for it raises the specter of race/racism. Such an acknowledgement works against the denial of race as a significant social factor, a denial which forms the core of Rodriguez's politics. Therefore, when Rodriguez uses racial arguments to steer the interpretation of his desire away from a homosexual register, he is obliged to further contain the racial implications of his arguments by introducing, characteristically, the rhetoric of class. His mother's remarks point the way for him.

In her anti-tanning rebuke, Rodriguez's mother includes a signifier of class: "You won't be satisfied till you end up like *los pobres* who work in the fields, *los braceros*" (113). Rodriguez pursues the class implications of her statement in an effort to further shift the sublimation of his homosexual desire from a race to a class register. He reflects:

> *Los pobres*—the poor, the pitiful, the powerless ones. But paradoxically also powerful men. They were the men with brown-muscled arms I stared at in awe on Saturday mornings when they showed up downtown like gypsies to shop at Woolworth's or Penney's. (113)

Rodriguez's initial attempt to racially defuse the erotic desire straining through his fascination undergoes a "meta-containment" by the assertion of putative class sympathy or solidarity. By the time he is finished, Rodriguez has taken two steps from the sexual interest he has been compelled initially to relate, so that the "real" issue underlying his sexual/racial interest becomes class:

> I considered the great victims of racism to be those who were poor and forced to do menial work. People like the farmworkers whose skin was dark from the sun. (118)

In this formulation, dark skin originates in a class-based experience—working in the sun—not from (I presume, biological) race. Rodriguez's homosexuality thus undergoes a kind of double transformation: his lack of sexual interest in women and desire for men, first represented as a "race thing," becomes, through his insight about the *braceros*, a "class thing."

One sees that at the points in his autobiography where racism most insistently impacts his life, Rodriguez introduces a diversionary narrative of heterosexual identity; the importance of racism is in this way reduced to its impact on Rodriguez's sexual development. Conversely, explaining his disinterest in heterosexuality as a product of racialized experience, Rodriguez steers the reader from considering another, explicitly sexual explanation for his sexual non-involvement with women. These intersectional discursive strategies are complicated further by the introduction of a "super-discourse" of class which further restricts any attempt to acknowledge racism or homosexuality. That this sublimation of homosexuality is carried out in his rumination over race; that, conversely, his sublimation of racial subordination is carried out in his rumination over sexuality; that a claim of class identification sutures the site at which the use of racial rhetoric threatens to coalesce into an anti-racist position, the complexity of this text speaks powerfully to the interlocking overdeterminations of sexuality, race and class experience in the United States. In the end, the swirl of Rodriguez's discourses settles not into a lack of clarity; the text reaches different degrees of resolution on each political count. Not surprisingly, things like superficial concern for the poor are resolved unambiguously (Who, after all, doesn't feel for the poor?). Issues such as racism and Rodriguez's homosexuality, which cannot be so neatly resolved, slip into artfully ambiguity.

I do not, of course, wish to trivialize the terror of the closet and the desperate rationalizations it can lead a gay person to undertake. Rodriguez's insertion of himself into the public sphere, however, earns him strenuous critique even on these painful issues. His success in exploiting these discourses in ways which uphold, at every level, the social status quo argues persuasively for the necessity of intersectional political analysis.

On a more personal level, Rodriguez's and Acosta's autobiographical writings also move me with compassion. In a world so hostile to homosexuality, it is no wonder that race or class "concerns" are frequently marshalled—often by lesbians and gay men themselves—along with innumerable other material and ideological forces, to keep queer people in the closet. What is lost to the closeted woman or man, however, likewise cannot be quantified. Understanding how writers make their sexuality (in)visible is no disservice to them, whether they are or consider themselves to be lesbian/gay or not. Exercises like mine are not meant to expose queers but to think about what it means to represent, textually or to oneself, homosexuality in the crowded space of identity formation. What emerges from an intersectional consideration of identity is always a better politics, a truer vision and, often, an understanding where there otherwise might simply be "ambiguity."

To close, I offer a moment from *The Autobiography of a Brown Buffalo*. Having returned to the home of his childhood, the narrator recalls an early misdeed. The significance, however, and his explanation of this deed remain strange, unless, perhaps, one "misreads" it through queer eyes:

> At the age of five I had a sickness known to both brown buffalos and sons of kings. How else is one to explain my grabbing the new rings my father had just purchased for my mother on their tenth anniversary and running out into the street with my brother at my heels? I had my face to the wind and heard his steps right behind me, so I threw them backwards without looking. And they were lost forever. (185)

Notes

1. Américo Paredes, *Folklore and Culture on the Texas-Mexican Border* (Austin: CMAS, 1993), 226.
2. Jose Antonio Villareal, *Pocho* (New York: Anchor, 1959), 177-8.
3. Juan Bruce-Novoa, "Homosexuality and the Chicano Novel," in *European Perspectives on Hispanic Literature in the United States*, ed. Genvieve Fabre (Houston: Arte Publico Press, 1988), 98.
4. Bruce-Novoa, 105.
5. Raymund A. Paredes, "The Evolution of Chicano Literature," in *Three American Literatures: Essays in Chicano, Native American, and Asian-American Literature for Teachers of American Literature*, ed. Houston A. Baker, Jr. (New York: The Modern Language Association of America, 1982), 74.
6. Raymund A. Paredes, "Mexican-American Literature: An Overview," in *Recovering the U.S. Hispanic Literary Heritage,* ed. Ramón A. Gutierrez and Genaro M. Padilla (Houston: Arte Publico Press, 1993), 48.
7. Surprisingly, Bruce-Novoa, while strongly arguing for the inclusion of Rechy in the Chicano canon, writes that in Rechy's fictional world "ethnicity ceases to be an explicit subject, becoming one alluded to through the metonymy of the author's background" (Bruce-Novoa, 101). I would disagree that autobio-

graphical "metonymy" can be understood as an "explicit" mark of ethnicity. In any case, Rechy's novels contain many references to the protagonist's upbringing on the Texas/Mexican border, his dark skin, his dangerous (i.e. ethnic) appeal on the streets, even his name in the case of *Numbers*, "Johnny Rio":

> Like a variable in an algebraic formula, ["Johnny Rio"'s] value is wholly determined by its context. In this case, the name of a "stock" Latin lover or exotic lead from some grade-B Hollywood film remains a fully motivated choice; in a specifically south Texan, Chicano context, it situates Johnny precisely on "el rio," the border, the fluid no-place between places whose symbolic and practical value as origin, as source of derivation, has been so productively articulated recently by Gloria Anzaldúa. (Ricardo L. Ortiz, "Sexuality Degree Zero: Pleasure and Power in the Novels of John Rechy, Arturo Islas, and Michael Nava," in Critical Essays: Gay and Lesbian Writers of Color, ed. Emmanuel S. Nelson (Binghamton, NY: Harrington Park Press, 1993), 116)

8. Jose David Saldívar's chapter on *The Rain God* in his book on Chicano/Latino literary practice also skirts any analysis of the gay content of the novel, focusing instead on the publishing industry's reluctance to publish the novel because they had pigeonholed it as "ethnic" (Jose David Saldívar, *The Dialectics of Our America* (Durham, NC: Duke University Press, 1991), 105-20). *Migrant Souls*, the sequel to *The Rain God*, also addresses male and female homosexuality, as does his final novel, *La Mollie and the King of Tears*. Recent excerpts from work that has emerged since Islas' death from complications of AIDS in 1991 are nothing short of graphic in their treatment of homosexuality (*Stanford Humanities Review* 2.2-3 (Spring 1992): 169-89).

9. Ramón Saldívar, *Chicano Narrative: The Dialectics of Difference* (Madison: The University of Wisconsin Press, 1990), 187.

10. Carl Gutiérrez-Jones, *Rethinking the Borderlands Between Chicano Culture and Legal Discourse* (Berkeley: University of California Press, 1995), 132. Further references are cited in the text.

11. He similarly discounts any real consideration of homosexual identity in his reading of Edward James Olmos' film, *American Me*.

12. Bruce-Novoa, 102.

13. Oscar Zeta Acosta, *The Autobiography of a Brown Buffalo* (NY: Vintage, 1989), 99. Further references are cited in the text.

14. Perhaps most amusing in this respect is his chance encounter with Liberace in *The Revolt of the Cockroach People*:

> "Mr. Brown? This man tells me you're running for Sheriff."
> "Yeah, I sure am."
> "Well...I hope you win."
> He reaches for my hand. I clasp his thumb. "This is the Chicano handshake," I say. He blushes and squeezes.
> "Hey, Mr. Liberace, will you vote for Zeta?"

The man looks at Victor and twinkles his green eyes. "Why of course."
(Oscar Zeta Acosta, The Revolt of the Cockroach People (NY: Vintage, 1989), 163. Further references are cited in the text.)

Commenting on this scene, Gutiérrez-Jones notes how "the moments of intense male bonding like that shared with Liberace" are contained by the "feverish anxiety" of the narrator's commitment "to heterosexual designs" (137).

15. The narrator also notes, somewhat less favorably, that his writing teacher "grounded [him] in the fundamentals of the short story by forcing [him] to read as much of the old fag Somerset Maugham as [he] could possibly tolerate" (146).

16. To be sure, the narrator emphasizes that his friendship with Jose has an artistic basis, not an ethnic, and certainly not a sexual one:
    Although the Polk District was filled with queens, butches and fags, Jose Ramon Lerma was one of the few homosexuals we tolerated at JJ's. Not simply because he had learned to keep the beast in his pockets, but because the only artist of the whole bunch of scags that had seriously studied at one time or another under Jack Jefferson at the San Francisco Art Institute. And because Jack had said he was the only one in the area destined for greatness, if the devil didn't get to him first. So we permitted him our holy heterosexual company. Without Jack's recommendation, we'd probably have let Jose starve. (47)
    In the end, however, artistic respect extends only so far, for soon, Acosta rids the bar of Jose in a bizarre, unexplained, sexually marked scene:
    I turn and see the Mexican mystic in all his glory. He's come out the toilet carrying his Big Mac coveralls in his hands...Except for my cousin Manuel, I have never seen such a long cock.
    By this time Sal is around the bar. While some dance and others scream, Sal takes Jose by the back of his railroad shirt and pushes him to the swinging doors. Jose goes without a word. Sal kicks him in the ass out into the dark. Everyone yells and claps and stomps their feet. (69)

17. He does, however, make satirical note of the man's "effeminate voice," "limp wrist," "waves of curly hair, carefully arranged to make him look ready for the opera," and closely spaced eyes, a sign the narrator claims is a flag for homosexuality.

18. The narrator makes other similar identifications ("guilt by association," to use Bruce-Novoa's phrase). The narrator's favorite hangout, JJ's, for example, is "caught between the Chinese expansion on one side and the gay liberation on the other" (43). Because his bar of choice is in the Polk District of San Francisco, the narrator regularly interacts with the "fancy-assed fags" who "are selling flowers on the corners" (36) and "young, blond fags with powder-blue eyes and soft shoes [who] skipped along arm-in-arm" (51). Likewise, at the beginning of *The Revolt of the Cockroach People*, the narrator describes his new home in Los Angeles:

a broken city filled with battered losers. Winos in tennies, skinny fags in tight pants and whores in purple skirts all ignore the world beyond the local bar, care about nothing except where the booze comes cheapest or the latest score on the radio. (23)

While his descriptions are homophobic, they nevertheless describe a man not only coexisting with homosexuals, but always conscious of his proximity to them.

19. Joe E. Rodriguez, "The Sense of Mestizaje in Two Latino Novels," *Revista Chicano-Riquena* 12.1 (1984): 62.
20. Eve Kosofsky Sedgwick, *Between Men: English Literature and Male Homosocial Desire* (New York: Columbia University Press, 1985), 91.
21. Ibid., 92-3.
22. In the narrator's car, Dr. Serbin's intrusion is marked by flirtation. The narrator remarks, "he winks at me. Did you see that? The crazy bastard actually winked at me" (36).
23. His most significant reappearance (which Américo Paredes might appreciate) is the narrator's drug-induced vision of him "sitting on top of Mr. Hemingway's grave" (120).
24. This scene's slide between homosocial and homosexual meaning is heightened in a later scene, possibly involving projection, in which the drugged narrator confuses the incident at Ruby's with a later one in which he sleeps with another man's wife. He muses:
    It all becomes clear now…I see it perfectly. He's pissed because I fucked Ruby. Down deep he's a repressed homosexual. That's why he wanted me to take his broad to bed. He wanted my cherry. (162)
25. Gutiérrez-Jones notes the Sedgwickian character of this strange scene:
    The "paranoid" awareness of the ultimately homosocial observation and control that applies to Zeta's political activities pervades the supposedly private escape to the Mexican brothel as well. Here the primary sexual encounter is framed by references to an anonymous male voyeur, a previous customer who was left unsatisfied. (138)
26. Hector Calderon, "To Read Chicano Narrative: Commentary and Metacommentary," *Mester*, 11.2 (1982): 7.
27. The narrator does not date earlier sexual activity like that with Carol, "an Italian living in an orange grove, who taught [him] about brassieres" (31). Neither does he give the date of his passive lesson in French kissing when "Madeline, a little Dutch girl, stuck her tongue down [his] throat" (31). The only early self-initiated sexual activity he describes involves his little sister: "Once I stuck my tongue in my sister Annie's mouth—I was practicing how to French kiss" (86).
28. In a single sentence paragraph he indicates without explanation that his participation in prostitution has ceased: "I started drinking more, I made no attempt to find a girlfriend. And after a time I even quit going to see Ruby" (113).

"Hey, Mr Liberace Will You Vote for Zeta?" 93

29. It must be noted that the long delayed act is rather brief:
    I explode upon contact. When it slides into the tightness, before I can even give her a chance, the blasted beast goes off like a rocket in the deep...my eyes close and I relax my entire body for the first time in over a year. Sometime later I hear the door slam and I am alone. But it doesn't matter. The sleep feels good and warm. I finally got a piece of ass. (65)
30. Vernon E. Lattin, *Minority Voices* 2.2 (Fall 1978): 38.
31. Genaro M. Padilla, "The Self as Cultural Metaphor in Acosta's *Autobiography of a Brown Buffalo*," *The Journal of General Education*, 35.4 (1984): 249.
32. For example, at the beginning of *The Revolt of the Cockroach People*–after his racial/sexual awakening–the narrator continues to claim, "I have...never touched a brown skin in tenderness" (47). As for the prostitutes who were supposed to have made him a true *indio* in the previous novel, he notes: "All through schools, jobs and bumming, I haven't even held the hand of a Mexican woman, excepting whores who are all the same anyhow" (29). The narrator becomes involved with three underage Chicanas who admire his political work, but even that relationship fails to live up to the racial/sexual utopian potential the narrator evokes at the end of the first novel. Gutiérrez-Jones comments:
    In the course of the novel, the only sexual relation with Chicanas established by Zeta takes on a complex, apparently symbolic form. The relation is constructed not with one partner but with three, simultaneously, and these three "have grown up together a sisters" (86). Far from obliquely representing anything like his own internal strife, these sisters appear to function as mechanically reproduced, mechanically exchangeable objects, sexual capital in all but name. (130)
33. Choosing Richard Rodriguez as a topic for discussion is a tricky political decision in itself. I strongly oppose virtually all the political positions Rodriguez has taken publicly. There are, however, a number of ways Rodriguez's writings form a near ideal object for the cultural criticism in which I wish to engage, foremost of which is how Rodriguez has been implicitly designated by the White dominated media and academy as the spokesperson for the Chicano community, despite the very low regard for him held by most prominent Chicana/o figures. An examination of Rodriguez's case sheds considerable light on the liberal media/academy's level of commitment to and awareness of the issues of concern to politically progressive Chicanos.
34. Richard Rodriguez, *Hunger of Memory: The Education of Richard Rodriguez* (New York: Bantam, 1982), 130. Further references are cited in the text.
35. Richard Rodriguez, "Huck Finn, Dan Quayle and the Value of Acceptance," *Los Angeles Times Magazine*, 20 September 1992, p. 33.
36. Cherrie Moraga, "Queer Aztlan: the Re-formation of Chicano Tribe," in *The Last Generation* (Boston: South End Press, 1993), 163.
37. Ilan Stavans, "The Latin Phallus," *Transition* 5.1 (1995): 57.

38. As recently as the July 20, 1995 *Los Angeles Times*, in an opinion piece, "'Group Rights': The Shameful Farce," Rodriguez has used the rhetoric of class politics to condemn race-based affirmative action efforts.
39. Despite his constant effort to downplay the role of racism in U.S. life, Rodriguez admits to having experienced racist attacks:

    I occasionally heard racial slurs. Complete strangers would yell out at me. A teenager drove past, shouting, "Hey, Greaser! Hey, Pancho!" Over his shoulder I saw the giggling face of his girl friend. A boy pedaled by and announced matter-of-factly, "I pee on dirty Mexicans." Such remarks would be said so casually that I wouldn't quickly realize that they were being addressed to me. When I did, I would be paralyzed with embarrassment, unable to return the insult...In all, there could not have been more than a dozen incidents of name-calling. That there were so few suggests that I was not a primary victim of racial abuse. But that, even today, I can clearly remember particular incidents is proof of their impact. Because of such incidents, I listened when my parents remarked that Mexicans were often mistreated in California border towns. And in Texas. I listened carefully when I heard that two of my cousins had been refused admittance to an "all-white" swimming pool. And that an uncle had been told by some man to go back to Africa. (117)

40. Yet another unfortunate consequence of Rodriguez's desire to rationalize a denied homosexuality is his sexist blaming of women, especially his mother, for the perpetuation of racist values. Rodriguez fails to consider the many ways that men, White, Chicano—men of all races—also participate in the maintenance of White supremacy.

    Acosta's narrator makes similar charges, accusing his father of generally authoritarian behavior, but specifically charging his mother with racism and with making him feel unattractive: "my mother had me convinced that I was obese, ugly as a pig and without any redeeming qualities whatsoever" (82). Like Rodriguez's mother, her insults have a racist character:

    My mother...always referred to my father as indio when he'd get drunk and accuse her of being addicted to aspirin. If our neighbors got drunk at the baptismal parties and danced all night to norteno music, they were "acting just like Indians." Once I stuck my tongue in my sister Annie's mouth—I was practicing how to French kiss-and my ma wouldn't let me back in the house until I learned to "quit behaving like an Indian." Naturally when Bob refused to get up and salute the American flag, he was just another one of "those lazy Indians." And when my sisters began to develop their teen-age fat, as chi chis expanded my mother was always after them to lay off the tortillas with hunks of colored margarine if they didn't want to end up marrying "some Indian." (86)

CHAPTER FIVE

"His Complexion was of a Tone I Want to Call Flesh-Colored"

In his introduction to the collection, *New Essays on* White Noise, Frank Lentricchia ends a list of possible reasons for the novel's having "broken through to a mass audience" with what he calls "the inevitable anecdotal reports." The first, which he "cannot resist sharing," goes this way: "In a course on contemporary fiction, one of my colleagues tells me that a student said to him, 'This is the first book in the course about me'."[1] Putting considerable stock, myself, in such anecdotes, I can't fault Lentricchia for sharing one. I mention this, however, because of an inverse reaction I had to a parallel experience around *White Noise*.

Some years ago, as a teaching assistant for a large lecture course on the American novel, I witnessed the young professor I worked under tell students words to the effect of "I think you'll all enjoy our next book, *White Noise*. We're finally going to read something about ourselves." While some of the students in my sections did enjoy the book and perhaps even identified with it, a number of them, particularly female students and students of color, did not. The latter two groups expressed various degrees of dislike and incomprehension, with, unfortunately, a consistent tone of doubt about diverging from the opinion of the literary authority before them in lecture. They wondered aloud about their ability as readers to understand and appreciate the "right things." This scenario highlights one of the dangers of conflating a particular experience—here, that of *White Noise*'s White, male narrator–with a universal one. When the professor named all in the room "we," he successfully interpellated, in the Althusserian sense, those in the room, but not with a resulting sense of connection between us all: quite the opposite. Many of the students whose life experience and desires closely matched those of the narrator recognized themselves "smoothly," whereas students coming from positions of significant difference tended to recognize the call to themselves in the professor's hailing, but with a concomitant sense of alienation. They accepted the imperative that they identify with the experience before them in the text, but did so with a simultaneous sense of ill-fit. Put differently, they accepted that they were among the "us" that *White Noise* was about, but, since what they read was unfamiliar or uninteresting, they had to see themselves as those of "us" who failed, who lacked something. This chapter explores the interpellating use of the "me" of Lentricchia's anecdotal student and the "us" of my own anecdote's professor. In the process, I consider the larger problem of identifying postmodern experience with that of Whites.[2]

Lentricchia devoted an issue of *South Atlantic Quarterly*, of which he was general editor, to Don DeLillo. This volume was later reissued as a book, *Introducing Don DeLillo*. Lentricchia subsequently edited a volume, *New Essays on* White Noise, for Cambridge University Press' high profile series on The American Novel, an important contemporary site for the maintenance of a canon of American literature. Whether or not DeLillo is worthy of aesthetic canonization is not, however, the concern of this chapter. The issue is, instead, the tropes through which the argument for DeLillo's importance is made. In Lentricchia and his collected critics' cases, the chief trope deployed is that of "universality." Throughout Lentricchia's introductions to both volumes, as well as most of the essays contained therein, it is simply taken for granted that DeLillo's representation of contemporary life in the U.S. is not only accurate, but complete. I will return in the last part of this chapter to these volumes. I begin, however, by interrogating the broader tendency, in which these two volumes on DeLillo participate: generalizing from White-authored texts. This practice, of course, does not originate with literary critics, but is, instead, the product of a history long dominated by Whites.

Since Marx's seminal, if scattered and brief, work on ideology, a fundamental aspect of social critique has been the recognition that dominant social groups maintain their power, not only through physical violence, but through the normalization of what, culturally, is specifically theirs. Marx argued that the values/interests of the ruling economic class are enforced not only through state violence but through the universalization on the ideological level of those values. A great body of Marxist literature on ideology exists, but other areas of cultural inquiry have made analogous use of this insight about the structure and function of ideology. Feminism, in particular, has revealed the penetration of patriarchal thought into all forms of human life. Feminist work on ideology demonstrates how, under patriarchy, men receive privilege not only through the explicit, often violent, advancement of their material interests, but through the articulation of things which are particular to or in the interest of men as "human" or "normal."

In recent decades, social movements as different as the lesbian/gay revolution and the organized struggle against ableism have used structurally analogous arguments in their political writings and activism, the latter deploying terms, for example, like "differently abled" to demonstrate that the "able" occupy only one position—albeit a massively privileged one—among many, just as the former has begun to use the term "heteronormativity," as opposed to "homophobia" or "heterosexism," to highlight the oppressive, false assumption that normal people are heterosexual. Whiteness, perhaps the final frontier of identity politics, has recently been looked at in a similar, critical fashion. Already important work in this field has been done and enables the writing of this chapter.

Crudely stated, like the bourgeoisie under capitalism, Whites control the U.S., if not global, economy and thus dominate major modes of representation. Film critic, Richard Dyer, who, in his groundbreaking study, *White*, perhaps has articulated most fully the set of problematics around representations of Whiteness, describes the normativization of Whiteness that goes on in everyday speech: "for most of the time white people speak about nothing but white people. It's just that we couch it in terms of 'people' in general."[3] Such a widespread "error" is only possible because of the material dominance of Whites. Dyer writes:

> we have not yet reached a situation in which white people and white cultural agendas are no longer in the ascendant. The media, politics, education are still in the hands of white people, still speak for whites while claiming–and sometimes sincerely aiming–to speak for humanity. (W, 3)

Dyer's "sometimes sincerely" points to one of the primary means by which the coercive character of White hegemonic practices achieves success. Whites, like all dominant groups, use ideology not so much to consistently celebrate themselves or denigrate those they mark as Other, but to align themselves with normative humanness. Dyer puts the case succinctly: "White power reproduces itself regardless of intention, power differences and goodwill, and overwhelmingly because it is not seen as whiteness, but as normal" (W, 10).

In the introduction to his indispensable historical study, *The Possessive Investment in Whiteness*, George Lipsitz also notes the hidden nature of normative White racial identity: "As the unmarked category against which difference is constructed, Whiteness never has to speak its name, never has to acknowledge its role as an organizing principle in social and cultural relations." "Whiteness," Lipsitz remarks, "is everywhere in U.S. culture, but it is very hard to see."[4] The denotative "invisibility" of Whiteness accounts for much of its strength. The unreflective, unintentional alignment of the culturally White with the human makes it difficult for Whites–or others under White hegemony–to see that this alignment is arbitrary and, in most cases, oppressive. Dyer writes:

> the position of speaking as a white person is one that white people now almost never acknowledge and this is part of the condition and power of whiteness: white people claim and achieve authority for what they

say by not admitting, indeed not realising, that for much of the time they speak only for whiteness. (W, xiv)

Indeed, to achieve a position of generally unopposed cultural dominance, White racial identity must be hidden.

The primary means through which this invisibility comes about, at least in Euro-American contexts, is Whiteness' operation as a "default" identification. In the field of representation, this default ensures that people/characters who are not racially specified, may safely be assumed to be White. Dyer notes that the absence of racial markers is the strongest signal of White identity:

> The sense of whites as non-raced is most evident in the absence of reference to whiteness in the habitual speech and writing of white people in the West. We (whites) will speak of, say, the blackness or Chineseness of friends, neighbors, colleagues, customers or clients, and it may be in the most genuinely friendly and accepting manner, but we don't mention the whiteness of the white people we know...all white people in the West do this all the time. (W, 2)

In this chapter, I look at the representation/concealment of Whiteness in DeLillo's *White Noise* and, more importantly, in a set of critical responses to it, to examine the process and ongoing nature of the translation of that which is particularly White to that which is characteristically human.

My move to reveal Whiteness in its specificity derives from the belief that representation plays a large role in how humans are socially organized and subsequently treated. The normalization of Whites into "people" has not only drastic epistemological, but practical implications for non-Whites. Dyer discusses how the "assumption that white people are just people...is not far off saying that whites are people whereas other colours are something else" (W,2). He therefore argues:

> the equation of being white with being human secures a position of power. White people have power and believe that they think, feel and act like and for all people; white people, unable to see their particularity, cannot take account of other people's; white people create the dominant images of the world and don't quite see that they thus construct the world in their own image; white people set standards of humanity by which they are bound to succeed and other bound to fail...For those in power in the West, as long as whiteness is felt to be the human condition, then it alone both defines normality and fully inhabits it (W, 9)

Recognizing that a disproportionate majority of literary criticism has been directed at texts by Whites, I am concerned that even critiquing such texts can reassert these texts' dominance, since criticism recenters them as objects of interest/importance. Whiteness is unavoidable, however. As Cuban American cultural critic Coco Fusco writes, it is necessary to in some ways address the Whiteness of Whites: "Racial identities are not only black, Latino, Asian, Native American, and so on; they are also white. To ignore white ethnicity is to redouble its hegemony by naturalizing it."[5] Compelled by this argument, I hope in this chapter to address Whiteness without problematically recentering it. To this end, I discuss Whiteness, not only in the multiethnic context of my book as a whole, but in a manner which I intend to work against White dominance of the cultural scene. In this respect I share Dyer's view:

> The point of seeing the racing of whites is to dislodge them/us from the position of power, with all the inequities, oppression, privileges and suffering in its train, dislodging them/us by undercutting the authority with which they/we speak and act in and on the world. (W, 2)

The primary way of challenging White hegemony in the world of representation involves denying its claim to universality. So while it might seem strange, I believe I must begin my analysis by racially identifying the central characters of *White Noise*. Jack Gladney and his family are White. Direct references to physical characteristics which might indicate "biological" race, however, are few.[6] This paucity of White racial reference functions, as I have suggested above, as the strongest sign of the Gladneys' European racial ancestry. The abundance of explicitly racialized references to non-White cultural products, practices and characters in the novel further confirms the White racial identity of the family.

All the White characters, for example, exhibit wide-ranging "multicultural" knowledge and interests. Even a very partial list of the novel's non-White racial references demonstrates the breadth and tone of the White characters' use of non-White racializations. Jay Murray Siskind, a colleague of Gladney, for example, is a veritable encyclopedia of Asian trivia. He claims, to give only a few examples, "Tibetans believe there is a transitional state between death and rebirth. Death is a waiting period, basically" (37); he admonishes, "Remember Lao Tse. 'There is no difference between the quick and the dead. They are one channel of vitality'" (150); he jokes, "Six hundred million Hindus stay home from work if the signs are not favorable that morning" (288). Other Whites in the novel exhibit similar knowledges of the non-White world. Lasher, another colleague of Gladney, suggests, "We ought to have an official Day of the Dead. Like the Mexicans" (216); Gladney's father in-law asks, "Didn't I read somewhere the Japanese go to Singapore? Whole planeloads of males. A remarkable people" (246). This flow of information about the world outside White America constitutes in large part the novel's titular "white noise," the infinite flow of information, whose ubiquity makes it the imperceptible backdrop for the individuated (White) objects moving within it.

These "knowledges," however, are less truths about non-White worlds than a means for maintaining a self-satisfied, but largely disengaged control over those worlds. A scene in which Babette reads aloud from tabloid magazines undercuts any supposition of the seriousness of these kinds of knowledge by sardonically indicating their possible origins. For this scene DeLillo invents a range of non-White comic oddities, including "reincarnation hypnotist Ling Ti Wan" and "Dr. Shiv Chatterjee, fitness guru and high-energy physicist" (142), as well as a "Japanese consortium" planning to "buy Air Force One and turn it into a luxury flying condominium with midair refueling privileges and air-to-surface missile capacity" (145).

This kind of superficial, "commodified," White knowledge of the racial Other typifies many kinds of contemporary U.S./European "multiculturalisms." Dyer notes:

> Postmodern multiculturalism may have genuinely opened up a space for the voices of the other, challenging the authority of the white West. But it may also simultaneously function as a side-show for white people who look on with delight at all the differences that surround them. (W, 4)

The sideshow function of multiculturalism is in full force in *White Noise*. In many instances, however, the White characters' "multiculturalism" goes beyond "sideshowism" to express a disturbing chauvinism, if not outright racism.

As the family discuss the anti-anxiety drug Dylar, for example, their conversation "comically" strays to race:

> "What do you know about Dylar?"
> "Is that the black girl who's staying with the Stovers?"
> "That's Dakar," Steffie said.
> "Dakar isn't her name, it's where she's from," Denise said. "It's a country on the ivory coast of Africa."
> "The capital is Lagos," Babette said. "I know that because a surfer movie I saw once where they travel all over the world." (80-1)

Gladney's doctor later expands on this joke, telling him, "he thought Dylar was an island in the Persian Gulf, one of those terminals crucial to the survival of the West" (180). In typical DeLillo fashion, information circuits bounce from ignorance to fact and back: funny, but only if one isn't troubled by the reduction of Black characters or nations to ciphers in non-Black people's word games.

In another conversation, the family pulls out sensationalizing myths as they discuss "exotic" diets:

> "Arabs eat glands."
> "The French eat glands," Babette said through gauze. "The Arabs eat eyes, speaking of eyes."
> "What parts?" Denise said.
> "The whole eye. The sheep eye."
> "They don't eat the lashes," Heinrich said.
> "Do sheep have lashes?" Steffie said. (158-9)

"His Complexion was of a Tone I Want to Call Flesh-Colored"   101

Culturally insensitive banter similarly structures a witty exchange about religion:

> "He's a Sunny Moslem," Orest said.
> "Iron City has some Sunnies out near the airport."
> "The Sunnies are mostly Korean. Except mine's an Arab, I think."
> I said, "Don't you mean the Moonies are mostly Korean?"
> "He's a Sunny," Orest said.
> "But it's the Moonies who are mostly Korean. Except they're not, of course. It's only the leadership." (267)

Another example takes on an ominous resonance today as the intensely conflicted nations of India and Pakistan face each other with nuclear weapons:

> "Around Christmas. I went to three drugstores and talked to the Indians behind the counters in the back."
> "I think they're Pakistanis."
> "Whatever." (179)

This chillingly indifferent "whatever" suggests the deeper character of the Gladneys' multiculturalist sensibilities and militates against viewing the presence of a non-White Other in the speech of *White Noise*'s White characters as a genuine expression of racial/ethnic pluralism.

Even discussions of disaster become occasions for White displays of wit:

> "Japan is pretty good for disaster footage," Alfonse said. "India remains largely untapped. They have tremendous potential with their famines, monsoons, religious strife, train wrecks, boat sinkings, etcetera. But their disasters tend to go unrecorded. Three lines in the newspaper. No film footage, no satellite hookup." (65)[7]

At best, Gladney and his family invoke non-White culture in a manner which, far from giving voice to non-White interests or experience, simply acts as a site for the White characters to show off their intellect or cleverness. At worst, their discursive use of race hints at a racist fear or dislike of non-Whites.[8]

This racist or xenophobic possibility is perhaps most evident in the novel's discourse around language. White characters' amusement with or interest in questions of language appear alongside expressions of fear or anger at racial/cultural difference. Babette, for example, demonstrates the former as she reads a tabloid aloud, changing "her voice to do dialogue": "Babette did the voices of Dr. Chatterjee and Patti Weaver. Her Chatterjee was a warm and mellow Indian-accented English, with clipped phrasing" (142-3). Another South Asian speaker (Gladney describes his voice as a "meticulous singsong"), however, occasions panic when Babette refers to Gladney's doctor's manner of speaking:

"What did Dr. Chakravarty say?"
"What could he say?"
"He speaks English beautifully. I love to hear him speak."
"What do you mean he loves to speak? Do you mean he takes every possible opportunity to speak? He's a doctor. He has to speak. In a very real sense you are paying him to speak. Do you mean he flaunts his beautiful English? He rubs your face in it?" (220)

Despite Gladney's admission that "Babette was right. He spoke English beautifully" (262), anxiety around non-Whites' use of language permeates his response. This anxiety about language difference appears in other places in the novel, as when, for example, Gladney notes the appearance, in his supermarket, of languages other than English:

> No everyone spoke English at the cash terminals, or near the fruit bins and frozen foods, or out among the cars in the lot. More and more I heard languages I could not identify much less understand, although the tall boys were American-born and the checkout women as well (40)

During a trip to the hardware store he reiterates this concern:

> I bought fifty feet of Manila hemp just to have it around, show it to my son, talk about where it comes from, how it's made. People spoke English, Hindi, Vietnamese, related tongues. (82)

The trivialization of non-White cultures becomes perhaps most serious, however, when the text moves from the White characters' "secondhand" representations of non-Whites to Gladney's direct narrative representation of them. The non-White characters who actually appear in *White Noise*, like the references to non-White people and objects, are, disseminated throughout the Gladneys' landscape as a kind of "white noise." DeLillo scatters nameless non-White bodies around the central White characters for comic or other tonal effects, from Gladney waking up to be stared at by "a wide-eyed Asian child" (154) to the family being greeted by "a group of turbaned schoolchildren, members of the local Sikh community, standing in the street with a hand-lettered sign: IRON CITY WELCOMES AREA EVACUEES" (160). An encounter on the street allows Gladney the chance to describe the general sensation non-White bodies engender in the White "everyone" of the town:

> The woman waved at Babette and headed toward us. She lived on our street with a teenage daughter and an Asian baby, Chun Duc. Everyone referred to the baby by name, almost in a tone of proud proprietorship, but no one knew who Chun belonged to or where he or she had come from. (39)

Gladney uses the mysterious/non-White and mysteriously-gendered Asian child to illustrate the White community's shared attitudes and protocols: people of color are something to have abstract pride in, but are not to be understood, even on the level of gender identity or family connection. This use of race is not unique in any way to Gladney; it is, in fact, the very convention for Whites. Dyer notes:

> white discourse implacably reduces the non-white subject to being a function of the white subject, not allowing her/him space or autonomy, permitting neither the recognition of similarities not the acceptance of differences except as a means for knowing the white self. (W, 13)

"Chun Duc" typifies this pattern, as "it" ties members of the White community together with the ennobling emotion of "pride," even as they lack interest enough to ascertain "its" sex or origin.

In her study of U.S. literature by White writers, *Playing in the Dark*, Toni Morrison explores how Black characters exist primarily, if not only, to explore, illustrate or serve White characters', readers' and writers' interests. Although primarily addressing the representation of African Americans, Morrison's book sheds light on how the representation of non-White Others functions in U.S. literature. She notes that U.S. writers typically use Black characters to "ignite critical moments of discovery or change or emphasis in literature not written by them."[9] Morrison examines how what she calls an "Africanist" presence plays itself out in literature by White Americans. She draws on Edward Said's notion of "Orientalism" to evoke a type of instrumentalist racializing of non-Whites. Like Said's "Oriental," Black characters in the writings of Whites are less representations of people than they are sites for exploring the White self:

> For the settlers and for American writers generally, this Africanist other became the means of thinking about body, mind, chaos, kindness, and love, provided the occasion for exercises in the absence of restraint, the presence of restraint, the contemplation of freedom and of aggression; permitted opportunities for the exploration of ethics and morality, for meeting the obligations of the social contract, for bearing the cross of religion and following out the ramifications of power. (PD, 47-8)

Morrison goes further, however, suggesting that the instrumental use of Black characters indicates a White interest in the maintenance of racial domination. In perhaps the most chilling passage of the book, Morrison describes the psychological value for Whites of the material subordination of Africanist Blacks:

> there is a lot of juice to be extracted from plummy reminiscences of "individualism" and "freedom" if the tree upon which such fruit hangs is a black population forced to serve as freedom's polar opposite: individualism is foregrounded (and believed in) when its background is stereotyped, enforced dependency. Freedom (to move, to earn, to learn, to be allied with a powerful center, to narrate the world) can be relished more deeply in a cheek-by jowl existence with the bound and unfree, the economically oppressed, the marginalized, the silenced. The

ideological dependence on racialism is intact and, like its metaphysical existence, offers in historical, political, and literary discourse a safe route into meditations on morality and ethics; a way of examining the mind-body dichotomy; a way of thinking about justice; a way of contemplating the modern world. (PD 64)

Non-White characters can provide such things to White readers, writers and characters only so long as the material conditions of non-Whites plausibly reflect those which are represented, and, conversely, as long as non-White characters do not escape their instrumental role for Whites to become objects of interest in their own right. To ensure that non-White characters "know their place," writers have generally resorted to "typing."

Dyer describes the process of typing in his essay, "The Role of Stereotypes":

> The type is any character constructed through the use of a few immediately recognizable and defining traits, which do not change or "develop" through the course of the narrative and which point to general, recurrent features of the human world...The opposite of the type is the novelistic character, defined by a multiplicity of traits that are only gradually revealed to us through the course of the narrative, a narrative which is hinged on the growth or development of the character and is centred upon the latter in her or his unique individuality, rather than pointing outwards to a world.[10]

In a White-dominated culture, Whites tend to represent non-Whites as types, whereas Whites "have the central and elaborated roles" (W,3); that is, they are represented as novelistic characters or, in the terminology of Orrin E. Klapp, cited by Dyer, "social types." Social types are "representations of those who 'belong' to society. They are the kinds of people that one expects, and is led to expect, to find in one's society, whereas stereotypes are those who do not belong" ("RS,"14). Defining Whites alone as social types through the use of novelistic characterizations has the ideological effect of marking non-Whites as "not part of society," despite a reality which might contradict such a claim:

> This is the most important function of the stereotype: to maintain sharp boundary definitions, to clearly define where the pale ends and thus who is clearly within and who clearly beyond it. Stereotypes insist on boundaries exactly at those points where in reality there are none. ("RS," 16)

In many places in *White Noise*, the psychological rationale for reducing non-White characters through stereotypification is evident. Gladney repeatedly points to the anxiety about what he and the other White characters generally see as the encroachment of non-White others. When his son, Heinrich, for example, brings home a friend, Orest, Gladney immediately conducts a "race check" on him, ending with a defensive non-sequitur:

> What kind of name is Orest? I studied his features. He might have been Hispanic, Middle Eastern, Central Asian, a dark-skinned Eastern European, a light-skinned black. Did he have an accent? I wasn't sure. Was he a Samoan, a native North American, a Sephardic Jew? It was getting hard to know what you couldn't say to people. (208)

Gladney goes through a similar "comic" mental survey when he finally encounters his nemesis, Mr. Grey:

> His nose was flat, his skin the color of a Planter's peanut. What is the geography of a spoon-shaped face? Was he Melanesian, Polynesian, Indonesian, Nepalese, Surinamese, Dutch-Chinese? Was he a composite?...Where was Surinam? (307)

The fact that Gladney shoots Grey seconds later mitigates what humor there might be in his speculations about race, and, this is what is most important: Gladney's desire to kill "Grey" tells of the extreme violence underlying the instrumental understanding of non-Whites by Whites.

At this point, I must turn, perhaps belatedly, to the role of irony in the text. As Lentricchia rightly notes in his introduction to *New Essays on White Noise*:

> In DeLillo's truly Swiftean satire, we're never sure what he himself believes or what he thinks of his characters. As in Swift, we're instead forced to rely on ourselves, to measure literary experience against our own sense of reality. (NEWN,13)

This masterful use of irony is perhaps the novel's greatest achievement. The interplay between DeLillo's simultaneous enshrinement and savage critique of the White middle class male psyche and lifespace, enabled by the irony of the text, accounts for much of the respect the novel has gained, both critically and commercially.

Unfortunately, *White Noise*'s irony has proven, I believe, to be its critical–in the sense of literary criticism–Achilles' heel. Despite the, one might say, crudeness of the novel's parodic intent (its narrator is, after all, the homicidal, sunglasses-wearing, hooded, non-German-speaking, founder of Hitler Studies), critics, when they turn to the text, seem to forget this crucial feature of the text. Even as they note DeLillo's skill with irony, they proceed to treat his text as a transparently mimetic of the postmodern world.[11]

Despite Lentricchia's own praise of the novel's irony, in his introduction to *New Essays* he sets the tone for such a stance, writing, for example, that DeLillo "insists in *White Noise*, as everywhere else in his work, upon a comprehensive canvas" (*NEWN*,7). Lentricchia imagines that DeLillo can be "comprehensive" because he also imagines that DeLillo can somehow step outside of his particular White identity. In the introduction to *Introducing Don DeLillo*, Lentricchia argues that writers like DeLillo:

> are not the sort who are impressed by the representative directive of the literary vocation of our time, the counsel to "write what you know." Writers in DeLillo's tradition have too much ambition to stay home. To leave home (I don't mean "transcend" it), to leave your region, your ethnicity, the idiom you grew up with. (IDD,2)

The same volume, however, includes an author interview conducted in "the picture-book Westchester suburb where DeLillo lives" (*IDD*,45). Given the relatively proximate identities of the White male heterosexual middle class writer DeLillo and the White male heterosexual middle class academic Gladney, it's not clear what Lentricchia means by DeLillo's "departure from self." It is far more salient, in fact, that DeLillo, in *White Noise*, is writing about a human experience which is personal, quite particular, not at all universal, and, in many ways, not much different than his own. DeLillo, at least in *White Noise*, does not leave—does not apparently even attempt to leave—his class, race or idiom. As eccentric as is Gladney, he remains closer racially to DeLillo than any of the non-Whites discussed or represented in *White Noise*.

Biography aside, however, the issue here is the specious critical argument for the typicality or universality of the Gladney family experience as American experience, and virtually all the critics here fall into this trap. In his own essay in *New Essays on* White Noise, "Tales of the Electronic Tribe," Lentricchia both puts Gladney in a lineage of U.S. ironic first-person White male narrators and asserts the utter representativeness of Gladney as a postmodern person:

> It probably can't be said too strongly: White Noise is a first-person narrative—a fact of literary structure that will turn out to be decisive for all that can be said about the book's take on contemporary America and the issues that cluster about the cloudy concept of postmodernism. Like Melville's Ishmael, Twain's Huck, and Fitzgerald's Nick Carraway, DeLillo's Jack Gladney is a sharp observer and commentator who at the same time participates—often to the reader's bewilderment—in an action which fatally shapes him, so that he will not understand with total lucidity what it is he observes, or who he himself really is, or the extent to which he, Jack Gladney, is the less than self-possessed voice of a culture that he would subject to criticism and satire. (NEWN, 92-3)

Lentricchia's rhetorical trick here is to claim that part of Gladney's limitation as a narrator lies in his inability to see how precisely he reflects his world. Thus, in an ironic gesture of his own, Lentricchia acknowledges Gladney's limitations, yet marks him simultaneously as the true voice of his culture, for Gladney's culture–which produced him–is limited in an identical way. In a deft rhetorical move the "unreliable" narrator Gladney becomes the ideal representor of our "unreliable" culture. Lentricchia finishes by naming this entire lineage of White male narrators as representative of their worlds:

> *Moby Dick, Huckleberry Finn, The Great Gatsby,* and *White Noise* are exemplary first person narratives in the American grain for the reason that their critical authority cannot be abstracted from their trapped and partially subverted first-person tellers(NEWN, 93).

Although the voices of Lentricchia's representative American narrators are "trapped and partially subverted," they nonetheless can be representative and constitute "the American Grain" in literature.

In Lentricchia's analysis, DeLillo's novel, true to its ironic spirit, "has it both ways." It seems to indict the White characters for their racist attitudes and manner of living, but, at the same time, it earns comic and aesthetic points for doing that which it putatively critiques its characters for doing: reducing non-White persons and culture to stereotypes, and thus reinforcing a White supremacist vision. While DeLillo's text may offer what one could, I suppose, call the "benefit" of this ironic doubleness around issues of race, many of the critics in DeLillo's collections don't come off so well. Far from articulating the particular and problematically empowered position of the White narrator and characters, they collectively offer support for the accuracy and comprehensiveness of *White Noise*'s treatment of postmodernity.

In his contribution to *New Essays,* "Whole Families Shopping at Night!," Tomas J. Ferraro writes: "Don DeLillo takes for his critical object of aesthetic concern the postmodern situation" (*NEWN,* 14). Ferraro can imagine that "the situation" of all living under postmodernity can be singularly identified for the same reason he can suggest that the "Gladneys are a representative contemporary family" (*NEWN,* 20); he implicitly elides the dominance of the White middle class family's social position with its ability to represent all contemporary families. He is, moreover, not content simply to argue for the representative character of the Gladneys at the present historical moment; Ferraro later suggests that the "innocence" of the Gladney's youngest son Wilder "is meant to augur the next stage of human experience" and "the advance of postmodernity itself" (*NEWN,* 28). U.S. Whites do and will, in his vision, define human experience itself.

Paul A. Cantor's contribution to this volume, "'Adolf, We Hardly Knew You'," though more critical of the narrator, still accepts Gladney's description of his world as accurate of the postmodern one as a whole: "Like all of DeLillo's work, *White Noise* portrays postmodern America" (*NEWN,* 41). Cantor equates the massively privileged life of the Gladneys with the lives of all under postmodernism:

> Here is the postmodern situation in capsule: everything, no matter how exotic or rare, is equally available, from all over the world, and indeed

> seemingly from all eras of history. Everything is neatly arranged, everything is labeled, and presumably, everything has a price. (NEWN, 43)

Needless to say, most people today do not have access to all things exotic and rare; many do not have those things "we" might think of as basic.

Cantor generalizes from the Gladneys in the area of political identity as well:

> With tongue in cheek, DeLillo suggests how attenuated America has become as a community, how little holds it together as a nation. Americans are no longer united by a common religion ("liturgies") or even by political forces ("laws"). All they have to unite them is a common culture, reflected in this communal rite-of-passage, but this common culture is itself highly attenuated, less a matter of values and beliefs than of what are usually called "lifestyles." These people do have something in common, but it is something superficial, a look, the image of sun-tanned athleticism cultivated in soft drink commercials. (NEWN, 50)

By accepting the *a priori* assumption of the Gladney's typicality, Cantor can then extrapolate from the Gladney family's situation larger truths about America's loss of communal ties. A more pluralist vision of the United States, however, makes the nostalgic claim about a lost national unity almost laughable. Middle class Whites, in their position of dominance, might have imagined or perhaps even have shared some commonalities in the past, but the radical subordination of non-Whites–from the extermination of American Indians and enslavement of Blacks to the exclusionary practices bent towards Latinos and Asian Americans–militates dramatically against some myth of a shared experience of American life. Suggestions, furthermore, of a "communal rite-of-passage" around the opening of liberal arts college campuses and a shared "image of sun-tanned athleticism" have little coherence once one moves out of the middle class White habitus.

Similarly, Cantor names the particular family problems of the Gladneys as the problem of all families in postmodern America:

> In *White Noise*, DeLillo views community as something that has become deeply problematic. The problem is clearest in the Gladney family, which can find little in common except watching television. Family solidarity is threatened in the contemporary world because it rests on a form of myth, a kind of error undermined by all the forces for enlightenment at work today (NEWN, 50)

Cantor even goes so far as to link this form of "enlightenment" to a desire for Nazism:

> Precisely because Nazism is irrational, because it rejects the Enlightenment, it fills a need in modern society that has lost its cohe-

siveness as rational inquiry undermines the mythic basis of communal solidarity (NEWN, 50)

While it may be that Nazism fills a White need in "modern society," the generalizing tendency outward from the Gladneys reveals itself most absurdly here. Non-White groups have not turned to Nazism in a need for the "irrational."

The remaining essay, by Michael Valdez Moses, similarly argues for the transcendental verisimilitude of the text, this time by comparing DeLillo's "philosophical" position with that of Martin Heidegger (a controversial figure whom Valdez Moses uncritically offers as a contemporary truthteller). Through recourse to the field of metaphysics, Valdez Moses is able to propose that *White Noise*, as philosophical text, can speak objectively about our world, that, for example, DeLillo is "reluctan[t] to become identified with any specific political agenda."[12] It is precisely the position of this chapter, however, that there is no such thing as an identity position without a politics.

Within their universalizing critiques, these critics do occasionally point to the specificity and privilege of *White Noise*'s central characters. Ferraro, for example, identifies DeLillo's "contribution" as one towards "understanding...suburban domesticity" (NEWN, 19); he also notes, "DeLillo does not bother to remind us that Disney World is no carnival for the underclasses, no fair for the local community, no animal farm for children but a national, *the* national, mecca for families" (NEWN, 36). Valdez Moses at one point asserts:

> DeLillo gives greater, or at least more explicit, emphasis to the economic forces at work. In a consumer culture, wealth provides the illusion of vulnerability. The power of technology allows its possessor or user to cover over the nearness and inevitability of personal death. The greater the wealth, the greater the quantum of technological power, the more distant personal death seems. (NEWN, 74)

I don't mean to suggest that these critics see the Gladneys as contemporary heroes or models. My argument is instead that even well-meaning, insightful critics such as these can–indeed will–fall into the trap of extrapolating from White to human experience without a conscious effort to see Whiteness in its specificity. Even at their best, these critics' efforts recall cultural critic bell hooks' comment on the Wim Wenders film, *Wings of Desire*: "It's another in a series where postmodern white culture looks at itself somewhat critically, revising here and there, then falling in love with itself all over again."[13]

To end, I return to the quotation with which I titled this chapter. Describing his German teacher, Gladney turns to the man's skin color, that most important metaphor of race. He says, "His complexion was of a tone I want to call flesh-colored" (32). Consistent, I believe, with his vision in the novel as a whole, Gladney expresses an understanding of the way that

Whites consolidate power in the United States and elsewhere by marking things human with the particularities of Whiteness. Jack knows that to call White people's skin "flesh-colored" is to colonize the very body we call human, to name "our" White skins human and skins that are not White something other than flesh. Jack also speaks frankly about the role of desire in the maintenance of the hegemony Whites achieve through this process of centering, normalizing, and universalizing Whiteness. He "wants" to call White skin "flesh." He tries to murder a man with the "skin the color of a Planter's peanut." That he does understand what he is doing, that he does tell his reader about it and that so many who read the text still see Gladney as the normative postmodern human being—all this speaks to a desire, not a mistake, for desire is an active process, to see Whites as human, to maintain the centrality, in our thinking and world, of Whites. Challenging this tendency will mean more than raising our consciousness. It will mean looking at what we want and what we will say and do for the things that we want.

Notes

1. Frank Lentricchia, ed., *New Essays on* White Noise (Cambridge: Cambridge University Press, 1991), 7. Further references are cited in the text with the abbreviation *NEWN*.
2. I use the term "White" in the sense described by historian George Lipsitz: "whiteness is, of course, a delusion, a scientific and cultural fiction that like all racial identities has no valid foundation in biology or anthropology. Whiteness is, however, a social fact, and identity created and continued with all-too-real consequences for the distribution of wealth, prestige, and opportunity" (George Lipsitz, *The Possessive Investment of Whiteness* (Philadelphia: Temple University Press, 1998), vii.
3. Richard Dyer, *White* (London: Routledge, 1997), 2. Further references are cited in the text with the abbreviation *W*.
4. Lipsitz, 1.
5. "Representing Whiteness: Seeing Wings of Desire," *Yearning: Race Gender and Cultural Politics*, bell hooks (Boston: South End Press, 1990), 171.
6. At one point a stranger describes a sensation of *deja vu* to Gladney, using physiological markers of Whiteness: "You were standing there...Your features incredibly sharp and clear. Light hair, washed-out eyes, pinkish nose, nondescript mouth and chin" (Don DeLillo, *White Noise* (New York: Viking, 1985), 163. Further references are cited in the text.). Gladney describes his current wife Babette in a way which also indicates that she is White: "Her hair is a fanatical blond mop, a particular tawny hue that used to be called dirty blond"(5). He later notes how Steffie, his daughter, has "a set of pale green eyes"(161). Significantly the only naming of a White character with the social

language of race comes in Gladney's climactic encounter with his nemesis, the ambiguously-raced Mr. Grey:

"Why are you here, white man?"
"To buy."
"You are very white, you know that?" (310)

7. The comically callous discussions about disasters in non-White areas find a telling parallel in a similar discussion about the class-valenced impact of disasters in the United States. Gladney reports:

These things happen to poor people who live in exposed areas. Society is set up in such a way that it's the poor and the uneducated who suffer the main impact of natural and man-made disasters. People in low-lying areas get the floods, people in shanties get the hurricanes and tornados. I'm a college professor. Did you ever see a college professor rowing a boat down his own street in one of those TV floods? We live in a neat and pleasant town near a college with a quaint name. These things don't happen in places like Blacksmith. (114)

He later adds: "I'm not just a college professor. I'm the head of a department. I don't see myself fleeing an airborne toxic event. That's for people who live in mobile homes out in the scrubby parts of the county, where the fish hatcheries are." (117). As always in the novel, the characters' intent, whether the object of critique or admiration, repulsive or comical, remains ironically ambiguous.

8. The White characters' real attitude toward multiculturalism, if not integration itself, are implied in a joke at the expense of bad taste television: "Babette tried to switch to a comedy series about a group of racially mixed kids who build their own communications satellite. She was startled by the force of our objections" (64).

9. Toni Morrison, *Playing in the Dark* (Cambridge, MA: Harvard University Press, 1992), viii. Further references are cited in the text with the abbreviation *PD*.

10. Richard Dyer, "The Role of Stereotypes," in *The Matter of Images* (London: Routledge, 1993), 13. Further references are cited in the text with the abbreviation "RS."

11. DeLillo is not entirely blameless in this respect, as his own comments in interviews show. For example, in a *Rolling Stone* interview, DeLillo was asked, "There seems to be a fondness in your writing, particularly in *White Noise*, for what might be described as the trappings of suburban middle class existence." Although the questioner specifies a particular habitus, and one implicitly White, DeLillo's answer frames his representation of U.S. life in generalizing terms:

I would call it a sense of the importance of daily life and of ordinary moments. In White Noise, in particular, I tried to find a kind of radiance in dailiness. Sometimes this radiance can be almost frightening. Other times it can be almost holy or sacred...Imagine someone from the third world who has never set foot in a place like that suddenly transported to an A&P in Chagrin Falls, Ohio. Wouldn't he be elated or frightened? Wouldn't he sense that something transcending is about to happen to him in the midst of all this brightness? So I think that's something that has been in the background of my work: a sense of something extraordinary hovering just beyond our touch and just beyond our vision. (Frank Lentricchia, ed., Introducing Don DeLillo, (Durham, NC: Duke University Press, 1991), 62. Further references will be included in the text with the abbreviation IDD.

DeLillo presumes that "someone from the third world" would experience the A&P in the holy way "we" would, again suggesting the universal character of the "suburban middle class" vision. That vision becomes "our" vision.

12. Michael Valdez Moses, "Lust Removed From Nature," *NEWN*, 84.
13. hooks, 165.

Bibliography

Acosta, Oscar Zeta. *The Autobiography of a Brown Buffalo*. New York: Vintage, 1989.

———. *The Revolt of the Cockroach People*. New York: Vintage, 1989.

Althusser, Louis. *Lenin and Philosophy and Other Essays*. New York: Monthly Review Press, 1971: 127-86.

Bruce-Novoa, Juan. "Homosexuality and the Chicano Novel." *European Perspective on Hispanic Literature in the United States*, edited by Genvieve Fabre. Houston: Arte Publico Press, 1988: 98-106.

Calderon, Hector. "To Read Chicano Narrative: Commentary and Metacommentary." *Mester* 11.2 (1982): 3-14.

Chan, Jeffrey Paul et al., eds., *Aiiieeeee!: An Anthology of Asian American Writers*. New York: Mentor, 1974.

Chan, Jeffrey Paul et al., eds., *The Big Aiiieeeee!*. New York: Meridian, 1991.

Chan, Jeffrey Paul and Frank Chin. "Racist Love." *Seeing Through Shuck*, edited by Richard Kostelanetz. New York: Ballantine, 1972: 65-79.

Chan, Sucheng. *Asian Americans: An Interpretive History*. Boston: Twayne Publishing, 1991.

Chang, Diana. Review of *Homebase*, by Shawn Wong. *Amerasia Journal* 8.1 (1981): 136-139.

Cheung, King-Kok. "The Woman Warrior versus The Chinaman Pacific: Must a Chinese American Critic Choose between Feminism and Heroism." In *Conflicts in Feminism*, eds. Marianne Hirsch and Evelyn Fox Keller. New York: Routledge, 1990: 234-251.

Chin, Frank, and Shawn Hsu Wong. Introduction. *Yardbird Reader*. Berkeley: Yardbird Publishing, 1974: vi-x.

Chu, Louis. *Eat a Bowl of Tea*. New York: Carol Publishing Group, 1990.

DeLillo, Don. *White Noise*. New York: Viking, 1985.

Dyer, Richard. *The Matter of Images*. London: Routledge, 1993.

Dyer, Richard. *White*. London: Routledge, 1997.

Fischer, Michael M.J.. "Ethnicity and the Post-Modern Arts of Memory." In *Writing Culture: The Poetics and Politics of Ethnography*, edited by James Clifford and George E. Marcus. Berkeley: University of California Press, 1986: 194-233.

Gutierrez-Jones, Carl. *Rethinking the Borderlands Between Chicano Culture and Legal Discourse*. Berkeley: University of California Press, 1995.

hooks, bell. *Talking Back*. Boston: South End Press, 1989.

———. *Yearning: Race, Gender, and Cultural Politics*. Boston: South End Press, 1991.

Hsiao, Ruth Y.. "Facing the Incurable: Patriarchy in *Eat a Bowl of Tea*." In *Reading the Literatures of Asian America*, edited by Shirley Geok-lin Lim and Amy Ling. Philadelphia: Temple University Press, 1992: 151-162.

Inada, Lawson Fusao. "Of Place and Displacement: The Range of Japanese-American Literature." In *Three American Literatures: Essays in Chicano, Native American, and Asian American Literature for Teachers of American Literature*, edited by Houston A. Baker, Jr.. New York: MLA, 1982: 254-265.

Islas, Arturo. *La Mollie and the King of Tears*. Albuquerque: University of New Mexico Press, 1996.

———. *Migrant Souls*. New York: William Morrow, 1990.

———. *The Rain God*. New York: Avon, 1991.

Kim, Elaine. *Asian American Literature: An Introduction to the Writings and Their Social Context*. Philadelphia: Temple University Press, 1982.

———. "'Such Opposite Creatures': Men and Women in Asian American Literature." *Michigan Quarterly Review* 29.1 (1990): 68-93.

Kim, Oggie. "Will the Ideal Role Model Please Stand Up?." *Bridge* 8.2 (1982): 27-28.

Kingston, Maxine Hong. *China Men*. New York: Vintage, 1989.

Laclau, Ernesto. *New Reflections of the Revolution of Our Time*. London: Verso, 1990.

———. *Politics and Ideology in Marxist Theory*. London: Verso, 1977.

Laclau, Ernesto and Chantal Mouffe. *Hegemony and Socialist Strategy.* London: Verso, 1985.

Lattin, Vernon E.. "Ethnicity and Identity in the Contemporary Chicano Novel." *Minority Voices* 2.2 (1978): 37-44.

Lentricchia, Frank, ed.. *Introducing Don DeLillo.* Durham, N.C.: Duke University Press, 1991.

———. ed.. *New Essays on* White Noise. Cambridge: Cambridge University Press, 1991.

Lipsitz, George. *The Possessive Investment in Whiteness.* Philadelphia: Temple Univeristy Press, 1998.

Moraga, Cherrie. *The Last Generation.* Boston: South End Press, 1993.

Morrison, Toni. *Beloved.* New York: Alfred A. Knopf, 1987.

———. *Playing in the Dark.* Cambridge, MA: Harvard University Press, 1992.

Nava, Michael. *Goldenboy.* Boston: Alyson, 1988.

———. *The Hidden Law.* New York: Ballantine, 1992.

———. *How Town.* New York: Ballantine, 1990.

Okada, John. *No-No Boy.* Seattle: University of Washington Press, 1976.

Omi, Michael, and Howard Winant. *Racial Formation in the United States: from the 1960's to the 1990's.* New York: Routledge, 1994.

Ortiz, Ricardo L.. "Sexuality Degree Zero: Pleasure and Power in the Novels of John Rechy, Arturo Islas, and Michael Nava." In *Critical Essays: Gay and Lesbian Writers of Color.* Ed. Emmanuel S. Nelson. Binghamton, NY: Harrington Park Press, 1993: 111-25.

Padilla, Genaro M.. "The Self as Cultural Metaphor in Acosta's *Autobiography of a Brown Buffalo.*" *The Journal of General Education*   35.4 (1984): 242-58.

Paredes, Americo. *Folklore and Culture on the Texas-Mexican Border.* Austin: CMAS, 1993.

———. *George Washington Gomez.* Houston: Arte Publico Press, 1990.

———. *"With His Pistol in His Hand": A Border Ballad and its Hero.* Austin: University of Texas Press, 1958.

Paredes, Raymund A.. "The Evolution of Chicano Literature." In *Three American Literatures: Essays in Chicano, Native American, and Asian-American Literature for Teachers of American Literature.* Ed. Houston A. Baker, Jr.. New York: The Modern Language Association of America, 1982: 33-79.

———. "Mexican-American Literature: An Overview." In *Recovering the US Hispanic Literary Heritage.* Ed. Ramon A. Gutierrez and Genaro M. Padilla. Houston: Arte Publico Press, 1993: 31-51.

Rechy, John. *City of Night*. New York: Grove Weidenfeld, 1963.

Rodriguez, Joe E.. "The sense of Mestizaje in Two Latino Novels." *Revista Chicano-Riquena* 12.1 (1984): 57-63.

Rodriguez, Richard. *Days of Obligation: An Argument with My Mexican Father*. New York: Viking, 1992.

———. *Hunger of Memory: The Education of Richard Rodriguez*. New York: Bantam, 1982.

Sakurai, Patricia A.. "The Politics of Possession: Negotiating Identities in *American in Disguise*, *Homebase*, and *Farewell to Manzanar*." *Critical Mass: A Journal of Asian American Cultural Criticism* 1.1 (1993): 39-56.

Saldivar, Jose David. *The Dialectics of Our America: Genealogy, Cultural Critique, and Literary History*. Durham: Duke University Press, 1991.

Saldivar, Ramon. *Chicano Narrative: The Dialectics of Difference*. Madison: The University of Wisconsin Press, 1990.

Sato, Gayle Fujita. "Momotaro's Exile: John Okada's *No-No Boy*." In *Reading the Literatures of Asian America*. Ed. Shirley Geok-lin Lim and Amy Ling. Philadelphia: Temple University Press, 1992: 239-258.

Sedgwick, Eve Kosofsky. *Between Men: English Literature and Male Homosocial Desire*. New York: Columbia University Press, 1985.

Stavans, Ilan. "The Latin Phallus." *Transition* 5.1 (1995): 48-68.

Villareal, Jose Antonio. *Pocho*. New York: Anchor, 1959.

Wong, Sau-ling Cynthia. "Ethnicizing Gender: An Exploration of Sexuality as Sign in Chinese Immigrant Literature." In *Reading the Literatures of Asian America*, edited by Shirley Geok-lin Lim and Amy Ling. Philadelphia: Temple University Press, 1992: 111-29.

Index

Acosta, Oscar Zeta, 12, 72–84, 88–89, 90–94n
Althusser, Louis, 2–4, 7
Anzaldúa, Gloria, 90n

Baker, Jr., Houston A., 45, 66n
Baldwin, James, 45, 66n
Bambara, Toni Cade, 45
Bradley, David, 44
Bruce-Novoa, Juan, 70, 74, 89n, 91n

Calderon, Hector, 78
Cantor, Paul A., 107–9
Chan, Jeffrey Paul, 16, 36n
Chan, Sucheng, 38n
Chang, Diana, 29
Cheung, King-Kok, 15–17, 37n
Chin, Frank, 1, 12, 15–18, 29, 36n
Chu, Louis, 36n
Cisneros, Sandra, 1

Davis, Arthur P., 44
Delany, Samuel, 44
DeLillo, Don, 12–13, 42, 95–110, 110–112n
Derrida, Jacques, 66n
Dyer, Richard, 97–99, 104

Ellison, Ralph, 42, 46
Eng, Fae Myenne, 35

Ferraro, Thomas J., 107, 109
Fischer, Michael M.J., 28–29
Flick, Arend, 65
Foucault, Michel, 6–7, 9
Fusco, Coco, 98

Gleason, William, 47, 48–49, 67n
Gutierrez-Jones, Carl, 72–73, 76, 92n

Hagedorn, Jessica, 35
Harris, Norman, 45, 66–67n
Hayward, Jennifer, 49–50, 52, 53
Heidegger, Martin, 109
Hemingway, Ernest, 69
hooks, bell, 13, 41, 109
Hsiao, Ruth Y., 36n
Husserl, Edmund, 66n
Hwang, David Henry, 36n

Inada, Lawson Fusao, 17–18, 36n
Islas, Arturo, 12, 71, 90n

Jen, Gish, 35
Johnson, Charles, 12, 42–65, 66–68n

Kadohata, Cynthia, 35
Kim, Elaine, 15–17, 29, 38n
Kim, Oggie, 28
Kingston, Maxine Hong, 1, 28, 35, 36n
Klapp, Orin E., 104

Laclau, Ernesto, 1–12
Laplanche, Jean, 10
Lattin, Vernon E., 83
LeClair, Tom, 43
Lentricchia, Frank, 95–96, 105–7
Lipsitz, George, 97, 110n
Little, Johnathan, 67n

Major, Clarence, 44
Marx, Karl, 96
Maugham, Somerset, 91n
Moraga, CherrRe, 84
Morrison, Toni, 1, 44–45, 103–4
Moses, Michael Valdez, 109
Mouffe, Chantal, 1, 5–9, 11–12

Nava, Michael, 71

Okada, John, 12, 17–29, 35, 37n
Olmos, Edward James, 72, 90n
Oritz, Ricardo, 90n

Padilla, Genaro M., 83
Paredes, AmJrico, 69
Paredes, Raymund, 70–71
Pontalis, J.B., 10

Rechy, John, 69–70, 89–90n
Reed, Ishmael, 1, 44
Riley, Clayton, 48
Rodriguez, Joe E., 76
Rodriguez, Richard, 12, 71, 84–88, 93–94n
Rushdy, Ashraf H.A., 42–43, 45–47

Said, Edward, 103
Sakurai, Patricia A., 34–35
SaldRvar, Jose David, 90n
SaldRvar, Ram\n, 71–72
Sato, Gayle K. Fujito, 37n
Sedgwick, Eve Kosofsky, 72–74, 76
Silko, Leslie Marmon, 1
Smith, Valerie, 41
Sung, Betty Lee, 36n

Tan, Amy, 35–36n

Villareal, Jose Antonio, 12, 69

Walker, Alice, 45, 66n
Wenders, Wim, 109
Williams, Sherley Anne, 41
Wong, Jade Snow, 36n
Wong, Sau-Ling Cynthia, 17
Wong, Shawn Hsu, 12, 17, 28–35, 36–39n